LUCIAN'S

ASSEMBLY OF THE GODS

An Intermediate Greek Reader

Greek Text with Running Vocabulary and Commentary

Evan Hayes

Steph

Lucian's *Assembly of the Gods*: An Intermediate Greek Reader: Greek Text with Running Vocabulary and Commentary

First Edition

© 2015 by Evan Hayes and Stephen Nimis

ISBN-10: 1940997143

ISBN-13: 9781940997148

Published by Faenum Publishing, Ltd.

Cover Design: Evan Hayes

Fonts: Garamond
         GFS Porson

editor@faenumpublishing.com

TABLE OF CONTENTS

φίλῳ εἰς ἀεί
Peter W. Rose

ACKNOWLEDGMENTS

The idea for this project grew out of work that we, the authors, did with support from Miami University's Undergraduate Summer Scholars Program, for which we thank Martha Weber and the Office of Advanced Research and Scholarship. Work on the series, of which this volume is a part, was generously funded by the Joanna Jackson Goldman Memorial Prize through the Honors Program at Miami University. We owe a great deal to Carolyn Haynes, and the 2010 Honors & Scholars Program Advisory Committee for their interest and confidence in the project.

The technical aspects of the project were made possible through the invaluable advice and support of Bill Hayes, Christopher Kuo, and Daniel Meyers. The equipment and staff of Miami University's Interactive Language Resource Center were a great help along the way. We are also indebted to the Perseus Project, especially Gregory Crane and Bridget Almas, for their technical help and resources. We also profited greatly from advice and help on the POD process from Geoffrey Steadman. All responsibility for errors, however, rests with the authors themselves.

INTRODUCTION

The aim of this book is to make *The Assembly of the Gods* by Lucian of Samosata (c. 120 CE –190) accessible to intermediate students of Ancient Greek. The running vocabulary and grammatical commentary are meant to provide everything necessary to read each page, so that readers can progress through the text, improving their knowledge of Greek while enjoying one of the most entertaining authors of antiquity. This short dialogue presents Momus, the god of blame, arguing that numerous gods and their entourages should be expelled from heaven for being fraudulent immigrants. These figures range from gods and heroes with a human parent to various "eastern" deities, whose unhellenic appearance and behavior is objectionable. A number of famous mythological stories are referred to as evidence of the unsuitability of various gods and goddesses to their home on Olympus, but not without implying that the behavior of Zeus himself is often petty and hypocritical.

Lucian's *The Assembly of the Gods* is a great text for intermediate readers. It is breezy and fun to read with relatively simple sentence structure. The diatribe of Momus sounds some of Lucian's favorite satirical and literary themes. It delineates the pettiness of quarrels over status and the hypocrisy of the powerful. It also provides implicit and explicit criticism of the verisimilitude and logic of traditional accounts of the gods. The language of Athenian democratic institutions is invoked throughout, which also humourously humanizes the Olympian figures.

LUCIAN OF SAMOSATA (C. 120 – 190 CE)

Little is known about the life of Lucian except what can be deduced from his numerous surviving works. By his own account, he was a professional rhetor, a "sophist," trained in public speaking. As such he is a good representative of the renaissance of Greek literature in the imperial period known as the "second sophistic." His Greek prose is patterned on the best Attic authors, a learned version of Greek that was more prestigious than the living lingua franca of the time, koine Greek, the Greek of the New Testament and public administration in the eastern half of the Roman Empire. His seventy works were transmitted in many manuscripts, indicating his continuous popularity in the Greek-speaking world. In the renaissance he was reintroduced to the Latin west and was widely read up to the beginning of the 20th century, when for various reasons he fell out of favor among classicists. Interest in Lucian has grown again, along with a greater interest in prose of the imperial period.

Menippean Satire and Lucian's Dialogues

Menippus of Gadara (3rd C. BCE) is the author of a number of satircal works in a mixture of prose and verse, all of which are lost. As a Cynic philosopher, he was famous for his biting wit and stinging criticism of contemporary society. The Roman author Varro (116 BCE – 27 BCE) wrote a large number of works in a similar vein, which he called *Saturae Menippeae (Menippean Satires)*, also no longer extant except for a few fragments. Lucian's dialogues are a part of this tradition and he makes explicit mention of Menippus in many instances. Dramatic settings in Olympus are a standard motif of Menippean satire, and *The Assembly* is one of four Lucianic dialogues set there (the other three being *Icaromenippus, Zeus Confounded, Zeus Rants*). There are also fragments of divine assemblies in the Roman satirists Lucilius and Varro, as well as the *Apocolocyntosis* of Seneca (c. 63 CE). This last work, a mixture of verse and prose, deals with the appropriateness of receiving the emperor Claudius into heaven, where many of the themes of Lucian's work can be found. J. Helm (1906) argued that all these examples stem from a work of Menippus of which Lucian's *The Assembly* is an imitation. However that may be, there is no doubt that the general spirit of Menippus' Cynic philosophy is present in *The Assembly*. Thus, while Momus rails humorously against various classes of suspect gods, his own snobbiness is also part of the satire. Schwartz (1965) finds evidence of more contemporary sources for *The Assembly*, such as Celsus, whose *True Discourse* (known to us only through later authors), suggests a view of the gods closer to the Epicurean school of philosophy.

The Assembly and the Antonine Reform of the Areopagus

Meanwhile, James Oliver (1980), has argued, based on epigraphical evidence, that the work has a more specific political inspiration. Two imperial proclamations have been preserved that make changes to the requirements for membership in the Areopagus committee in Athens in the second century. One is dated 165 CE and the second 174 CE. The first, a letter from Marcus Aurelius and Lucius Verus, restricts the membership based on birth, representing this action as a restoration of the more traditional rules that had been abandoned; the second, a letter from Marcus Aurelius alone, relaxes the rules that had been imposed in the first instance. Oliver speculates that the stricter rules for membership proved too difficult to impose due to an intervening plague and a new war against the Germans, both of which impacted old aristocratic families in Athens.

In this context, Lucian's dialogue seems to parallel the earlier imperial declaration. The revised rules responded to the influx of "unworthy elements" into the prestigious ranks of Areopagites, and sought to reimpose an older standard and set up a committee to investigate the credentials of current members. The diatribe of Momus in *The Assembly* presents a similar set of arguments against foreigners and half-breeds, and his proposal at the end of the dialogue echoes the official language of Athenian democratic institutions. It is thus fair to assume that the impulse for writing *The Assembly* was this imperial decree and the reaction that it produced among Athenians at the time. As usual, it is difficult to be sure what Lucian's specific political agenda is in this dialogue, if any, but its historical context suggests that Lucian has been motivated to write by current events, not just by general philosophical interests or literary precedents.

Lucian's Gods and Greek Paideia

In a recent evaluation of the evidence, Spickerman (2010) concludes that alluding to the contemporary imperial reform of the Areopagus is only one objective of *The Assembly* and other dialogues that include divine assemblies. Lucian is also making a conservative and moralizing critique of his contemporary world in comparison to the classical ideal. This is reinforced by Spickerman's analysis of Lucian's view of religion and the traditional gods in *The Assembly* and related dialogues. Spickerman (2009) observes a hierarchy among Lucian's gods: most important and universal are Homer's gods, along with their Roman equivalents; next come the deities of Asia Minor and Syria, reinterpreted in terms of Greek institutions and traditions, among whom are the Egyptian deities; then follow Mithras, Sabazios and other phenomena of Lucian's time, gods coming from outside the circle of Greco-Roman culture and rarely Hellenized. Finally come those beyond the bounds of proper religion, especially the oracle cults, which were generally criticized in the Second Sophistic. Spickerman concludes that Lucian maintains a philosopher's scepticism about the efficacy of the gods, being particularly resistant to magic, superstition and oracles. At the same time Lucian sees the Homeric gods as as a central element of Greek identity and *paideia*; despite his mockery of the contradictions and absurdities of that tradition, it must be defended. This *paideia*, Spickerman notes, is not just a *techne*, but rather a way of life which harmonized philosophy, rhetoric and sophistic performance.

The Greek Text

The Greek text is that of K. Jacobitz (1896), which has been digitized by the Perseus Project and made available with a Creative Commons license, as is our text. Here and there we have made minor changes to the text in the name of readability. This is not a scholarly edition; for that one should turn to the OCT of Macleod.

Select Bibliography

Branham, R. Bracht. *Unruly Eloquence: Lucian and the Comedy of Traditions.* Harvard University Press: Cambridge, 1987.

Deferrari, R. J. *Lucian's Atticism.* Hackert: Amsterdam, 1969.

Follet, S. "Lettre de Marc-Aurèle aux Atheniens (EM 13366): Nouvelles lectures et interpretations," *Revue de Philologie* 53 (1979) 29-43.

Helm, R. *Lucian und Menipp.* Leipzig: G. B. Teubner, 1906.

Householder, F. W. *Literary Quotation and Allusion in Lucian.* King's Crown Press: Morningside Heights, 1941.

Oliver, James H. "The Actuality of Lucian's *Assembly of the Gods.*" *The American Journal of Philology*, Vol. 101.3 (Autumn, 1980), 304-313.

Spickermann, Wolfgang. "Lukian von Samosata und die fremden Götter." *Archive für Religionsgeschichte* 11 (2009), 229-261.

----------------. "Lukian von Samosata und die Volksversammlungen," in edd. Vera V. Dement'eva and Tassilo Schmitt, *Volk und Demokratie im Altertum.* (Göttingen: Ruprecht, 2010), 159-173.

Schwartz, J. *Biographie de Lucien de Samosate.* Latomus 83: Brussels, 1965.

Whitmarsh, T. *The Second Sophistic.* Oxford: Oxford University Press, 2005.

----------------. *Beyond The Second Sophistic.* Berkeley: University of California Press, 2013.

How to use this book

The page by page vocabularies gloss all but the most common words. We have endeavored to make these glossaries as useful as possible without becoming fulsome. Words occurring frequently in the text can be found in an appendix in the back, but it is our hope that most readers will not need to use this appendix often.

The commentary is almost exclusively grammatical, explaining subordinate clauses, unusual verb forms, and idioms. Brief summaries of a number of grammatical and morphological topics are interspersed through the text as well, and there is a list of verbs used by Lucian that have unusual forms in an appendix. The principal parts of those verbs are given there rather than in the glossaries.

An Important Disclaimer:

This volume is a self-published "Print on Demand" (POD) book, and it has not been vetted or edited in the usual way by publishing professionals. There are sure to be some factual and typographical errors in the text, for which we apologize in advance. The volume is also available only through online distributors, since each book is printed when ordered online. However, this publishing channel and format also account for the low price of the book; and it is a simple matter to make changes when they come to our attention. For this reason, any corrections or suggestions for improvement are welcome and will be addressed as quickly as possible in future versions of the text.

Please e-mail corrections or suggestions to editor@faenumpublishing.com.

About the Authors:

Evan Hayes is a recent graduate in Classics and Philosophy at Miami University and the 2011 Joanna Jackson Goldman Scholar.

Stephen Nimis is an Emeritus Professor of Classics at Miami University and Professor of English and Comparative Literature at the American University in Cairo.

ABBREVIATIONS

abs.	absolute	mid.	middle
acc.	accusative	neg.	negative
act.	active	neut.	neuter
adj.	adjective	nom.	nominative
adv.	adverb	obj.	object
aor.	aorist	opt.	optative
attrib.	attributive	part.	participle
circum.	circumstantial	pass.	passive
dat.	dative	perf.	perfect
dir.	direct	pl.	plural
f.	feminine	plupf.	pluperfect
fut.	future	pot.	potential
gen.	genitive	pres.	present
i.e.	*id est* ("that is")	pred.	predicate
imper.	imperative	s.	singular
impf.	imperfect	sc.	*scilicet* ("supply")
ind.	indirect	st.	statement
inf.	infinitive	subj.	subjunctive
m.	masculine	voc.	vocative

ΛΟΥΚΙΑΝΟΥ
ΘΕΩΝ ᾿ΕΚΚΛΗΣΙΑ

Lucian's
Assembly of the Gods

ΘΕΩΝ ΕΚΚΛΗΣΙΑ

ΖΕΥΣ: Μηκέτι τονθορύζετε, ὦ θεοί, μηδὲ κατὰ γωνίας συστρεφόμενοι πρὸς οὓς ἀλλήλοις κοινολογεῖσθε, ἀγανακτοῦντες εἰ πολλοὶ ἀνάξιοι μετέχουσιν ἡμῖν τοῦ συμποσίου, ἀλλ' ἐπείπερ ἀποδέδοται περὶ τούτων ἐκκλησία, λεγέτω ἕκαστος ἐς τὸ φανερὸν τὰ δοκοῦντά οἱ καὶ κατηγορείτω. σὺ δὲ κήρυττε, ὦ Ἑρμῆ, τὸ κήρυγμα τὸ ἐκ τοῦ νόμου.

ΕΡΜΗΣ: Ἄκουε, σίγα. τίς ἀγορεύειν βούλεται τῶν τελείων θεῶν οἷς ἔξεστιν; ἡ δὲ σκέψις περὶ τῶν μετοίκων καὶ ξένων.

ἀγανακτέω: to feel irritation
ἀγορεύω: to speak publicly
ἀκούω: to hear
ἀλλήλων: one another
ἀνάξιος, -ον: unworthy
ἀποδίδωμι: to grant, allow
βούλομαι: to wish (+ *inf.*)
γωνία, ἡ: a corner, angle
δοκέω: to seem
ἐκκλησία, ἡ: an assembly
ἐπείπερ: seeing that
Ἑρμῆς, -οῦ, ὁ: Hermes
θεός, ὁ: God
κατηγορέω: to argue, accuse
κήρυγμα, -ατος, τό: a proclamation

κηρύττω: to proclaim
κοινολογέομαι: to take counsel with
μετέχω: to partake of
μέτοικος, ὁ: a metic, foreigner living in Athens
μηκέτι: no more, no longer
νόμος, ὁ: custom, law, ordinance
ξένος, ὁ: a foreigner
σιγάω: to be silent
σκέψις, -εως, ἡ: a viewing
συμπόσιον, τό: a drinking-party
συστρέφω: to curl up
τέλειος, -α, -ον: finished, complete
τονθορύζω: to mutter, babble
φανερός, -ά, -όν: visible, manifest

ἀγανακτοῦντες: pres. part. causal, "because being annoyed"

εἰ ... μετέχουσιν: noun clause after ἀγανακτοῦντες, "annoyed *whether they share in*" + gen.

ἀποδέδοται: perf. of ἀπο-δίδωμι, "if an assembly *has been granted*"

λεγέτω: pres. imper. 3 s., "let each speak!"

οἱ: dat. with δοκοῦντα, "the things seeming *to him*" i.e. his opinions

κατηγορείτω: pres. imper. 3 s., "let each argue"

τὸ κήρυγμα: cognate acc., "proclaim *the proclamation*"

οἷς ἔξεστιν: relative clause, "to whom it is permitted"

ΜΩΜΟΣ: Ἐγὼ ὁ Μῶμος, ὦ Ζεῦ, εἴ μοι ἐπιτρέψειας εἰπεῖν.

ΖΕΥΣ: Τὸ κήρυγμα ἤδη ἐφίησιν· ὥστε οὐδὲν ἐμοῦ δεήσει.

ΜΩΜΟΣ: Φημὶ τοίνυν δεινὰ ποιεῖν ἐνίους ἡμῶν, οἷς οὐκ ἀπόχρη θεοὺς ἐξ ἀνθρώπων αὐτοῖς γεγενῆσθαι, ἀλλ', εἰ μὴ καὶ τοὺς ἀκολούθους καὶ θεράποντας αὐτῶν ἰσοτίμους ἡμῖν ἀποφανοῦσιν, οὐδὲν μέγα οὐδὲ νεανικὸν οἴονται εἰργάσθαι. ἀξιῶ δέ, ὦ Ζεῦ, μετὰ παρρησίας μοι δοῦναι εἰπεῖν· οὐδὲ γὰρ ἂν ἄλλως δυναίμην, ἀλλὰ

ἀκόλουθος, -ον: following
ἄλλως: otherwise
ἀξιόω: to think worthy of, ask
ἀποφαίνω: to show forth, display
ἀποχράω: to be sufficient
δεῖ: it is necessary
δεινός, -ή, -όν: fearful, terrible
δίδωμι: to give
δύναμαι: to be able
ἔνιοι, -α,: some
ἐπιτρέπω: to turn towards, allow

ἐργάζομαι: to work, labour
ἐφίημι: to send to, allow
ἤδη: already
θεράπων, -οντος, ὁ: a attendant
ἰσότιμος, -ον: held in equal honour
κήρυγμα, -ατος, τό: a proclamation
Μῶμος, ὁ: Momus, god of scorn
νεανικός, -ή, -όν: fresh, new
παρρησία, ἡ: freespokenness
τοίνυν: therefore, accordingly
φημί: to declare, make known

ἐπιτρέψειας: aor. opt. in future less vivid protasis, "if you would allow me" + inf.

ἐφίησιν: pres. of ἐπι-ἵημι, "already *allows*"

δεήσει: future of δεῖ, "there will be no need"

ποιεῖν: pres. inf. in ind. st., "I say that some *are doing*"

οὐκ ... ἀλλ': "not (only) .. but (also)"

αὐτοῖς: intensive agreeing with οἷς and the subject of γεγενῆσθαι, "that *they themselves* become"

γεγενῆσθαι: perf. inf. after ἀπόχρη, "not enough *to have become*"

ἀποφανοῦσιν: fut. instead of subj. indicating something undesirable, "unless *they shall show* their followers" i.e. *cause* them to be

ἡμῖν: dat. after ἰσοτίμους, "equal in rank *to us*"

εἰργάσθαι: perf. inf. in ind. st. after οἴονται, "they suppose *that they have done nothing*"

δοῦναι: aor. inf. complementing ἀξιῶ, "I ask you *to grant*"

εἰπεῖν: aor. inf. complementing δοῦναι, "grant me *to speak*"

δυναίμην: pres. opt. pot., "I would not be able"

πάντες με ἴσασιν ὡς ἐλεύθερός εἰμι τὴν γλῶτταν καὶ
οὐδὲν ἂν κατασιωπήσαιμι τῶν οὐ καλῶς γιγνομένων:
διελέγχω γὰρ ἅπαντα καὶ λέγω τὰ δοκοῦντά μοι ἐς τὸ
φανερὸν οὔτε δεδιώς τινα οὔτε ὑπ' αἰδοῦς ἐπικαλύπτων
τὴν γνώμην: ὥστε καὶ ἐπαχθὴς δοκῶ τοῖς πολλοῖς καὶ
συκοφαντικὸς τὴν φύσιν, δημόσιός τις κατήγορος ὑπ'
αὐτῶν ἐπονομαζόμενος. πλὴν ἀλλ' ἐπείπερ ἔξεστιν καὶ
κεκήρυκται καὶ σύ, ὦ Ζεῦ, δίδως μετ' ἐξουσίας εἰπεῖν,
οὐδὲν ὑποστειλάμενος ἐρῶ.

αἰδώς, -οῦς, ὁ: a sense of shame
γλῶττα, -ας, ἡ: the tongue
γνώμη, ἡ: a thought
δέδια: to fear (*perf.*)
δημόσιος, -α, -ον: public
διελέγχω: to refute, charge
ἐλεύθερος, -α, -ον: free
ἔξεστι: it is allowed
ἐξουσία, ἡ: power or authority
ἐπαχθής, -ές: heavy, ponderous

ἐπείπερ: seeing that
ἐπικαλύπτω: to cover up
ἐπονομάζω: to name or call
κατασιωπάω: to be silent about
κατήγορος, ὁ: an accuser
κηρύττω: to proclaim
συκοφαντικός, -ή, -όν: slanderous
ὑποστέλλω: to hold back
φανερός, -ά, -όν: visible, evident
φύσις, ἡ: nature

τὴν γλῶτταν: acc. of respect., "I am free *with my tongue*"
κατασιωπήσαιμι: aor. opt. pot., "I would not be silent about" + gen.
τὰ δοκοῦντά: pres. part., "*the things that seem true* to me"
ὑπ' αἰδοῦς: expressing cause, "because of respect"
τὴν φύσιν: acc. of respect, "sycophantic *in nature*"
δημόσιός τις κατήγορος: nom. pred., "being called *a popular prosecutor*"
πλὴν ἀλλ': strong adversative, "but"
κεκήρυκται: perf. of κηρύττω, "since it has been proclaimed"
εἰπεῖν: aor. inf. after δίδως, "you grant *to speak*"
ὑποστειλάμενος: aor. part. mid. of ὑπο-στέλλω, "*having held back* not at all"

Potential Optatives

The optative with ἄν expresses potentiality, with a range of possible meanings:

ἡδέως ἂν οὖν ἐροίμην σε: "I would like to ask"

οὐ γὰρ ἂν ἄλλως εἴποιμι: "I could not speak otherwise"

οὐδὲ γὰρ ἂν ἄλλως δυναίμην: "I would not be able otherwise"

Πολλοὶ γάρ, φημί, οὐκ ἀγαπῶντες ὅτι αὐτοὶ
μετέχουσι τῶν αὐτῶν ἡμῖν ξυνεδρίων καὶ εὐωχοῦνται ἐπ'
ἴσης, καὶ ταῦτα θνητοὶ ἐξ ἡμισείας ὄντες, ἔτι καὶ τοὺς
ὑπηρέτας καὶ θιασώτας τοὺς αὐτῶν ἀνήγαγον ἐς τὸν
οὐρανὸν καὶ παρενέγραψαν, καὶ νῦν ἐπ' ἴσης διανομάς
τε νέμονται καὶ θυσιῶν μετέχουσιν, οὐδὲ καταβαλόντες
ἡμῖν τὸ μετοίκιον.

ἀγαπάω: to treat with affection	καταβάλλω: to pay down
ἀνάγω: to lead up	μετέχω: to partake of (+ gen.)
διανομή, ἡ: a distribution	μετοίκιον, τό: the tax paid by metics
εὐωχέω: to entertain sumptuously	νέμω: to distribute, dispense
ἥμισυς, -εια,-υ: half	ξυνέδριον, τό: a council
θιασώτης, -ου, ὁ: a companion	οὐρανός, ὁ: heaven
θνητός, -ός, -όν: mortal	παρεγγράφω: to enroll illegally
θυσία, ἡ: an offering	ὑπηρέτης, -ου, ὁ: a servant
ἴσος, -η, -ον: equal to, the same as	φημί: to declare, make known

---

ὅτι αὐτοὶ μετέχουσι: noun clause after ἀγαπῶντες, "not content *that they themselves participate in*" + gen.

ἐπ' ἴσης (sc. μοίρας): "according to an equal (share)" i.e. equally

ἐξ ἡμισείας (sc. μοίρας): "of half (portion)" i.e. "being *half* human"

ἀνήγαγον: aor. of ἀνα-άγω, "in addition *they led up*"

παρενέγραψαν: aor. of παρα-ἐν-γράφω, "they fraudulently registered"

νέμονται: pres. mid., "they distribute among themselves" i.e. they take possession of

καταβαλόντες: aor. part., "not even *having paid down*"

τὸ μετοίκιον: from μετα-οῖκος, the resident alien tax paid in Athens by foreigners

---

Note the different meanings of the word αὐτός:

1. The nominative forms of the word without the definite article are always intensive (= Latin *ipse*): αὐτός: he himself; αὐτοί, they themselves.

   οὐκ ἀγαπῶντες ὅτι <u>αὐτοὶ</u> μετέχουσι: "not content that *they themselves* share"

   The other cases of the word are also intensive when they modify a noun or pronoun, either without the definite article or in predicative position:

   εἰ δὲ ἐξῆν καὶ πρὸς <u>αὐτὸν</u> σὲ τῇ παρρησίᾳ χρῆσθαι: "if it were necessary to speak freely against *you yourself*"

2. Oblique cases of the word, when used without a noun or a definite article, are the unemphatic third person pronouns: *him, them*, etc.:

   ὑπ' <u>αὐτῶν</u> ἐπονομαζόμενος: "being named *by them*"; πρὸς <u>αὐτὸν</u>: "toward *him*"

3. Any case of the word with an article in attributive position means "the same":

   τὸν αὐτὸν τρόπον: "the same manner"

ΖΕΥΣ: Μηδὲν αἰνιγματῶδες, ὦ Μῶμε, ἀλλὰ σαφῶς καὶ διαρρήδην λέγε, προστιθεὶς καὶ τοὔνομα, νῦν γὰρ ἐς τὸ μέσον ἀπέρριπταί σοι ὁ λόγος, ὡς πολλοὺς εἰκάζειν καὶ ἐφαρμόζειν ἄλλοτε ἄλλον τοῖς λεγομένοις. χρὴ δὲ παρρησιαστὴν ὄντα μηδὲν ὀκνεῖν λέγειν.

ΜΩΜΟΣ: Εὖ γε, ὦ Ζεῦ, ὅτι καὶ παροτρύνεις με πρὸς τὴν παρρησίαν: ποιεῖς γὰρ τοῦτο βασιλικὸν ὡς ἀληθῶς καὶ μεγαλόφρον, ὥστε ἐρῶ καὶ τοὔνομα.

ὁ γάρ τοι γενναιότατος οὗτος Διόνυσος ἡμιάνθρωπος ὤν, οὐδὲ Ἕλλην μητρόθεν ἀλλὰ Συροφοίνικός τινος

αἰνιγματώδης, -ες: riddling, dark
ἀληθῶς: truly
ἄλλοτε: at another time, at other times
ἀπορρίπτω: to throw away, put away
βασιλικός, -ή, -όν: royal, kingly
γενναῖος, -α, -ον: noble
διαρρήδην: expressly, distinctly
Διόνυσος, ὁ: Dionysus
εἰκάζω: to make like to
Ἕλλην, -νος, ὁ: a Greek
ἐρῶ: I will say or speak
ἐφαρμόζω: to fit to
ἡμιάνθρωπος, ὁ: a half-man

μεγαλόφρων, -ον: high-minded
μέσος, -η, -ον: middle, in the middle
μητρόθεν: from the mother
ὀκνέω: to shrink from (+ *inf.*)
ὄνομα, τό: a name
παροτρύνω: to urge
παρρησία, ἡ: freespokenness, frankness
παρρησιαστής, -οῦ, ὁ: a free speaker
προστίθημι: to put to, supply
σαφής, -ές: clear, plain
Συροφοῖνιξ, -ικος, ὁ: a Syro-phoenician
τοι: surely
χρή: it is necessary

προστιθεὶς: pres. part., "*supplying also the name*"

ἀπέρριπταί: perf. of **ἀπορρίπτω**, "your account *has been cast out*"

ὡς πολλοὺς εἰκάζειν καὶ ἐφαρμόζειν: pres. inf. in result clause, "so that many are guessing and cause to fit"

ἄλλοτε ἄλλον: object of **ἐφαρμόζειν** also in a result clause, "many fit *now one now another* to the words"

ὄντα: pres. part. causal agreeing with the acc. subj. of **ὀκνεῖν**, "you, *since you are* a free speaker"

λέγειν: pres. inf. after **ὀκνεῖν**, "shrink *from saying*"

βασιλικὸν ... μεγαλόφρον: acc. adverbial, "royally and generously"

Διόνυσος: Dionysus was the son of Zeus and Semele, the daughter of Cadmus

Συροφοίνικος: although Cadmus founded Thebes, he was from the Phoenician city of Tyre

ἐμπόρου τοῦ Κάδμου θυγατριδοῦς, ἐπείπερ ἠξιώθη
τῆς ἀθανασίας, οἷος μὲν αὐτός ἐστιν οὐ λέγω, οὔτε
τὴν μίτραν οὔτε τὴν μέθην οὔτε τὸ βάδισμα· πάντες
γάρ, οἶμαι, ὁρᾶτε ὡς θῆλυς καὶ γυναικεῖος τὴν φύσιν,
ἡμιμανής, ἀκράτου ἔωθεν ἀποπνέων· ὁ δὲ καὶ ὅλην
φατρίαν ἐσεποίησεν ἡμῖν καὶ τὸν χορὸν ἐπαγόμενος
πάρεστι καὶ θεοὺς ἀπέφηνε τὸν Πᾶνα καὶ τὸν Σιληνὸν καὶ
Σατύρους, ἀγροίκους τινὰς καὶ αἰπόλους τοὺς πολλούς,
σκιρτητικοὺς ἀνθρώπους καὶ τὰς μορφὰς ἀλλοκότους·

ἄγροικος, -ον: rustic
ἀθανασία, ἡ: immortality
αἰπόλος, ὁ: goatherd
ἄκρατος, -ον: unmixed, sheer
ἀλλόκοτος, -ον: strange, monstrous
ἀξιόω: to think worthy of (+ gen.)
ἀποπνέω: to breathe forth
ἀποφαίνω: to show forth, display
βάδισμα, -ατος, τό: walk, gait
γυναικεῖος, -α, -ον: womanish
εἰσποιέω: to introduce
ἔμπορος, -ον: a wayfarer
ἐπάγω: to bring on
ἔωθεν: from morning
ἡμιμανής, -ές: half-mad
θῆλυς, -εῖα, -υ: feminine

θυγατριδοῦς, -οῦ, ὁ: a grandson
Κάδμος, ὁ: Cadmus
μέθη, ἡ: strong drink
μίτρα, ἡ: a belt or girdle
μορφή, ἡ: form, shape
οἷος, -α, -ον: such as, what sort
ὅλος, -η, -ον: whole, entire
Πάν, ὁ: Pan
πάρειμι: to be present
Σάτυρος, ὁ: a Satyr
Σιληνός, ὁ: Silenus
σκιρτητικός, -ή, -όν: skittish, unruly
φατριά, ἡ: a clan
φύσις, ἡ: nature
χορός, ὁ: a round dance

ἠξιώθη: aor. pass., "he was deemed worthy of" + gen.

οἷος ... ἐστιν: ind. question, "say *what sort he is*"

οὔτε ... οὔτε ... οὔτε: note the use of *praeteritio* to mention the things he says he will *not* mention

τὴν φύσιν: acc. of respect, "feminine *in nature*"

ἀκράτου (sc. οἴνου): gen. after ἀποπνέων, "smelling *of unmixed* wine" i.e. having it on his breath

ὁ δὲ: answering to οἷος μὲν above, "*but in addition he* introduced his whole clan"

ἀπέφηνε: aor. of ἀπο-φαίνω, "he made to appear" i.e. caused to be seen as gods

Πᾶνα: sometimes represented as the son of Dionysus (or Zeus or Hermes) but comparable in any case to other half-animals like the satyrs

Σιληνὸν: associated with Dionysus as well by his semi-bestial nature

Σατύρους: the satyrs were regularly associated with Dionysus because of their outlandish behavior

ὧν ὁ μὲν κέρατα ἔχων καὶ ὅσον ἐξ ἡμισείας ἐς τὸ κάτω
αἰγὶ ἐοικὼς καὶ γένειον βαθὺ καθειμένος ὀλίγον τράγου
διαφέρων ἐστίν, ὁ δὲ φαλακρὸς γέρων, σιμὸς τὴν ῥῖνα,
ἐπὶ ὄνου τὰ πολλὰ ὀχούμενος, Λυδὸς οὗτος, οἱ δὲ
Σάτυροι ὀξεῖς τὰ ὦτα, καὶ αὐτοὶ φαλακροί, κεράσται,
οἷα τοῖς ἄρτι γεννηθεῖσιν ἐρίφοις τὰ κέρατα ὑποφύεται,
Φρύγες τινὲς ὄντες· ἔχουσι δὲ καὶ οὐρὰς ἅπαντες. ὁρᾶτε
οἵους ἡμῖν θεοὺς ποιεῖ ὁ γεννάδας;

αἴξ, αἰγός, ὁ: a goat
ἄρτι: just, exactly
βαθύς, -εῖα, -ύ: deep,high
γένειον, τό: a beard
γεννάδας, -ου, ὁ: a noble
γεννάω: to beget, engender
γέρων, -οντος, ὁ: an old man
διαφέρω: to carry across, differ
ἔοικα: to seem (*perf.*)
ἔριφος, ὁ: a young goat, kid
ἡμίσεια, ἡ: a half
καθίημι: to send down, let fall
κάτω: down, below
κέρας, -ατος, τό: the horn of an animal
κεράστης, -ου, ὁ: horned

Λυδός, ὁ: a Lydian
οἷος, -α, -ον: such as, what sort
ὀλίγος, -η, -ον: few, little, scanty, small
ὄνος, ὁ: an ass
ὀξύς, -εῖα, -ύ: sharp, keen
ὁράω: to see
οὐρά, ἡ: the tail
οὖς, ὠτός, τό: the ear
ὀχέω: to uphold, sustain, carry
ῥίς, ἡ: the nose
σιμός, -ή, -όν: snub-nosed, flat-nosed
τράγος, ὁ: a he-goat
ὑποφύω: to make to grow up
φαλακρός, -ά, -όν: bald

ὧν ὁ μὲν ... ὁ δὲ ... οἱ δὲ: "of whom one ... etc." taking up the three just mentioned in order
ἐξ ἡμισείας: "*from the middle* down"
ἐοικὼς: perf. part., "*looking like* a goat"
καθειμένος: perf. part. of κατα-ἵημι, "*having sent down* a beard"
ὀλίγον: acc. of extent with adverbial force, "differing *to a small degree*"
τὴν ῥῖνα: acc. of respect, "a monkey *in nose*"
τὰ πολλὰ: acc. of extent with adverbial force, "most of the time"
ὀχούμενος: pres. part. pass., "being carried"
τὰ ὦτα: acc. of respect, "sharp *in ears*" i.e. with pointed ears
οἷα ... ὑποφύεται: "horned, *like those that grow*"
γεννηθεῖσιν: aor. part. pass. dat. of γεννάω, "to kids newly *born*"
ὁ γεννάδας: "the noble one," referring ironically to Dionysus

9

Εἶτα θαυμάζομεν εἰ καταφρονοῦσιν ἡμῶν οἱ ἄνθρωποι ὁρῶντες οὕτω γελοίους θεοὺς καὶ τεραστίους; ἐῶ γὰρ
λέγειν ὅτι καὶ δύο γυναῖκας ἀνήγαγεν, τὴν μὲν ἐρωμένην
οὖσαν αὐτοῦ, τὴν Ἀριάδνην, ἧς καὶ τὸν στέφανον
ἐγκατέλεξε τῷ τῶν ἄστρων χορῷ, τὴν δὲ Ἰκαρίου τοῦ
γεωργοῦ θυγατέρα. καὶ ὃ πάντων γελοιότατον, ὦ θεοί,

ἀνάγω: to lead up	ἐράω: to love
Ἀριάδνη, ἡ: Ariadne, daughter of Minos	θαυμάζω: to wonder, marvel
ἄστρον, τό: the stars	θυγάτηρ, -τέρος, ἡ: a daughter
γέλοιος, -α, -ον: laughable	Ἰκάριος: Icarian
γεωργός, ὁ: a farmer	καταφρονέω: to despise
γυνή, -αικός, ἡ: a woman	στέφανος, ὁ: that which surrounds
δύο: two	τεράστιος, -ον: monstrous
ἐάω: to allow	χορός, ὁ: a round dance
ἐγκαταλέγω: to set X (*acc.*) among Y (*dat.*)	

εἰ καταφρονοῦσιν: ind. question after θαυμάζομεν, "wonder *whether they despise*"

ἐῶ γὰρ λέγειν: "I allow to say," i.e. I pass over in silence, another *praeteritio*

ἀνήγαγεν: aor. of ἀνα-άγω, "that *he brought up*"

ἐρωμένην: pres. part. acc. pred., "the one being *his beloved*"

Ἀριάδνην: after being abandoned by Theseus, Ariadne was rescued by Dionysus, who married her

τὸν στέφανον: the garland of Ariadne became the constellation *Corona*

τὴν δὲ Ἰκαρίου: Erigone, the daughter of Icarius, to whom Dionysus taught the secrets of making wine

---

Defective Verbs

The principal parts of some verbs come from completely different words. Sometimes there are more than one form for a specific tense, in which case one will usually be preferred. Here are some important examples:

Present	Future	Aorist	Perfect	Aorist Passive	Translation
ἔρχομαι	εἶμι	ἦλθον	ἐλήλουθα		to go
	ἐλεύσομαι				
φέρω	οἴσω	ἤνεγκα	ἐνήνοχα	ἠνέχθην	to bear, carry
		ἤνεγκον			
λέγω	ἐρέω	εἶπον	εἴρηκα	ἐρρήθην	to speak
	λέξω	ἔλεξα	λέλεγμαι	ἐλέχθην	

καὶ τὸν κύνα τῆς Ἠριγόνης, καὶ τοῦτον ἀνήγαγεν, ὡς μὴ
ἀνιῷτο ἡ παῖς εἰ μὴ ἔξει ἐν τῷ οὐρανῷ τὸ ξύνηθες ἐκεῖνο
καὶ ὅπερ ἠγάπα κυνίδιον. ταῦτα οὐχ ὕβρις ὑμῖν δοκεῖ καὶ
παροινία καὶ γέλως; ἀκούσατε δ' οὖν καὶ ἄλλους.

ἀγαπάω: to love, be fond of
ἀκούω: to hear
ἀνάγω: to lead up
ἀνιάω: to grieve, distress
γέλως, ὁ: laughter
Ἠριγόνη, ἡ: Erigone
κυνίδιον, τό: a little dog, puppy

κύων, κύνος, ὁ: a dog
ξυνήθης, -ες: habitual, customary
οὐρανός, ὁ: heaven
παῖς, ἡ: a child
παροινία, ἡ: drunken violence
ὕβρις, ἡ: wanton violence

τὸν κύνα: after Icarius was killed, Erigone's dog led her to the site of the corpse
ὡς μὴ ἀνιῷτο: pres. opt. in neg. purpose clause, "lest she be distressed"
εἰ μὴ ἔξει: fut. of ἔχω indicating an undesirable premise, "unless she shall have"
ὅπερ ἠγάπα: impf., "whom she used to love"
ταῦτα: the subject of δοκεῖ, "do *these things* not seem?"

Imperatives

There are many more imperatives in Lucian's dialogues, so it is worth reviewing their forms. Here is the regular conjugation of the present and first aorist illustrated with λύω:

Present Imperative

Number	Person	Active	Middle / Passive
Singular	2nd	λῦε	λύου (from ε-σο)
	3rd	λυέτο	λυέσθω
Plural	2nd	λύετε	λύεσθε
	3rd	λυόντων	λυέσθων

Aorist Imperative

Number	Person	Active	Middle	Passive
Singular	2nd	λῦσον	λῦσαι	λύθητι
	3rd	λυσάτω	λυσάσθω	λυθήτω
Plural	2nd	λύσατε	λύασθε	λύθητε
	3rd	λυάντων	λυάσθων	λυθέντων

The imperatives of second aorist verbs regularly take the same endings as the present imperative: λάβε, λαβέτω, etc.

The perfect imperative is rare.

ΖΕΥΣ: Μηδέν, ὦ Μῶμε, εἴπῃς μήτε περὶ Ἀσκληπιοῦ μήτε περὶ Ἡρακλέους· ὁρῶ γὰρ οἷ φέρῃ τῷ λόγῳ. οὗτοι γάρ, ὁ μὲν αὐτῶν ἰᾶται καὶ ἀνίστησιν ἐκ τῶν νόσων καὶ ἔστιν «πολλῶν ἀντάξιος ἄλλων,» ὁ δὲ Ἡρακλῆς υἱὸς ὢν ἐμὸς οὐκ ὀλίγων πόνων ἐπρίατο τὴν ἀθανασίαν· ὥστε μὴ κατηγόρει αὐτῶν.

ΜΩΜΟΣ: Σιωπήσομαι, ὦ Ζεῦ, διὰ σέ, πολλὰ εἰπεῖν ἔχων. καίτοι εἰ μηδὲν ἄλλο, ἔτι τὰ σημεῖα ἔχουσι τοῦ πυρός. εἰ δὲ ἐξῆν καὶ πρὸς αὐτὸν σὲ τῇ παρρησίᾳ χρῆσθαι, πολλὰ ἂν εἶχον εἰπεῖν.

ἀθανασία, ἡ: immortality
ἀνίστημι: to make to stand up, raise up
ἀντάξιος, -ον: worth just as much as
Ἀσκληπιός, ὁ: Asclepius
εἶπον: to speak, say
ἔξεστι: it is possible
Ἡρακλέης, ὁ: Heracles
ἰάομαι: to heal, cure
κατηγορέω: to accuse (+ gen.)
νόσος, ἡ: sickness, disease, malady
ὀλίγος, -η, -ον: few, little, scanty, small

ὁράω: to see
παρρησία, ἡ: freespokenness
πόνος, ὁ: work, labor
πρίαμαι: to buy
πῦρ, πυρός, τό: fire
σημεῖον, τό: a sign, a mark, token
σιωπάω: to be silent
υἱός, ὁ: a son
φέρω: to bear
χράομαι: to use (+ dat.)

μηδέν ... εἴπῃς: aor. subj. in prohibition, "speak nothing!"
Ἀσκληπιοῦ: Asclepius was the son of Apollo and Coronis, a human
Ἡρακλέους: Heracles also had a mortal mother, Alcmene
οἷ: dat. expressing place to which "I see *whither* you are going"
πολλῶν ἀντάξιος ἄλλων: "worth as much as many others," said of Machaon the healer in *Iliad* 11.514
οὐκ ὀλίγων πόνων: gen. of value, "bought *for not few pains*"
μὴ κατηγόρει: pres. imper., "and so *don't accuse*"
εἰπεῖν: aor. inf. after ἔχων, "being able *to say*"
τοῦ πυρός: "signs *of fire*" Heracles was consumed by fire and Asclepius struck by lightning. These σημεῖα perhaps recall the branding of slaves.
ἐξῆν: impf. in present contrafactual protasis, "if it were possible" + inf.
παρρησίᾳ: dat. of means with χρῆσθαι, "to use *free speech*"
ἂν εἶχον: impf. ind. in present contrafactual apodosis, "I would be able" + inf.

ΖΕΥΣ: Καὶ μὴν πρὸς ἐμὲ ἔξεστιν μάλιστα. μῶν δ' οὖν κἀμὲ ξενίας διώκεις;

ΜΩΜΟΣ: Ἐν Κρήτῃ μὲν οὐ μόνον τοῦτο ἀκοῦσαι ἔστιν, ἀλλὰ καὶ ἄλλο τι περὶ σοῦ λέγουσιν καὶ τάφον ἐπιδεικνύουσιν· ἐγὼ δὲ οὔτε ἐκείνοις πείθομαι οὔτε Ἀχαιῶν Αἰγιεῦσιν ὑποβολιμαῖόν σε εἶναι φάσκουσιν. ἃ δὲ μάλιστα ἐλεγχθῆναι δεῖν ἡγοῦμαι, ταῦτα ἐρῶ.

Τὴν γάρ τοι ἀρχὴν τῶν τοιούτων παρανομημάτων καὶ τὴν αἰτίαν τοῦ νοθευθῆναι ἡμῶν τὸ ξυνέδριον σύ, ὦ Ζεῦ, παρέσχες θνηταῖς ἐπιμιγνύμενος καὶ κατιὼν παρ'

Αἴγιοι, οἱ: the Aegians	κάτειμι: to go down
αἰτία, ἡ: a charge, accusation	Κρήτη, ἡ: Crete
ἀκούω: to hear	μόνον: only
ἀρχή, ἡ: beginning, source	νοθεύω: to adulterate
Ἀχαιόι, οἱ: the Achaeans	ξενία, ἡ: status of an alien
δεῖ: to be necessary	ξυνέδριον, τό: a council
διώκω: to pursue, accuse	παρανόμημα, -ατος, τό: an illegal act
ἐλέγχω: to disgrace, put to shame	παρέχω: to furnish, provide
ἔξεστι: it is possible	πείθω: to persuade
ἐπιδείκνυμι: to show, prove	τάφος, ὁ: a tomb
ἐπιμίγνυμι: to mix with	τοι: let me tell you, surely, verily
ἐρῶ: I will say or speak	τοιοῦτος, -αύτη, -οῦτο: such as this
ἡγέομαι: to think	ὑποβολιμαῖος, -α, -ον: substituted by stealth
θνητός, -ή, -όν: mortal	φάσκω: to say, affirm, assert

καὶ μὴν: "let me tell you!"

ξενίας: genitive of the charge, "accusing me *of being an alien*"

μῶν: "surely not" expecting a negative answer

Κρήτῃ: in the fusion of Minoan and Mycenean myth, Crete became the site of Zeus' birth and death

ἔστιν: note the accent, "it is possible" + inf.

Αἰγιεῦσιν: dat. pl. after πείθομαι, "nor believe *the Aegians* of Achaea"

ὑποβολιμαῖόν: acc. pred., "say you are *a foundling*," a version of Zeus' birth not mentioned elsewhere

φάσκουσιν: pres. part. agreeing with Αἰγιεῦσιν, "the Aegians *who say*"

ἐλεγχθῆναι: aor. pass. inf. after δεῖν, "necessary *to be censured*"

τοῦ νοθευθῆναι: aor. pass. inf. articular gen., "cause *of the adulterating*"

παρέσχες: aor., "*you provided* the beginning"

ἐπιμιγνύμενος: pres. part. instrumental, "by mingling with" + dat.

Lucian

αὐτὰς ἐν ἄλλοτε ἄλλῳ σχήματι, ὥστε ἡμᾶς δεδιέναι μή
σε καταθύσῃ τις ξυλλαβών, ὁπόταν ταῦρος ᾖς, ἢ τῶν
χρυσοχόων τις κατεργάσηται χρυσὸν ὄντα, καὶ ἀντὶ
Διὸς ἢ ὅρμος ἢ ψέλιον ἢ ἐλλόβιον ἡμῖν γένῃ.

πλὴν ἀλλὰ ἐμπέπληκάς γε τὸν οὐρανὸν τῶν
ἡμιθέων τούτων· οὐ γὰρ ἂν ἄλλως εἴποιμι. καὶ τὸ
πρᾶγμα γελοιότατόν ἐστιν, ὁπόταν τις ἄφνω ἀκούσῃ

ἄλλοτε: at another time, at other times	ξυλλαμβάνω: to capture
ἄλλως: in another way or manner	ὅρμος, ὁ: a cord, chain
ἄφνω: unawares, of a sudden	οὐρανός, ὁ: heaven
γέλοιος, -α, -ον: laughable	πρᾶγμα, -ατος, τό: a deed, matter
ἐλλόβιον, τό: an earring	σχῆμα, -ατος, τό: form
ἐμπίπλημι: to fill	ταῦρος, ὁ: a bull
ἡμίθεος, ὁ: a half-god, demigod	χρυσός, ὁ: gold
καταθύω: to sacrifice	χρυσόχοος, ὁ: a goldsmith
κατεργάζομαι: to effect by labour	ψέλιον, τό: an armlet or anklet

ἐν ἄλλοτε ἄλλῳ σχήματι: "in one or another form"

δεδιέναι: perf. inf. in result clause, "so that we fear"

μή σε καταθύσῃ: aor. subj. in clause of fearing, "fear *that someone will sacrifice you*,"
Zeus became a bull to seduce Europa

ᾖς: pres. subj. in general temporal clause, "when(ever) *you are*"

κατεργάσηται: aor. subj. in clause of fearing, "fear that someone *will work you*"

ὄντα: pres. part. acc., "you *being* gold," Zeus became golden rain to seduce Danae

γένῃ: aor. subj. of γίγνομαι in clause of fearing, "fear *that you will become*"

πλὴν ἀλλὰ: strong adversative, "but"

ἐμπέπληκάς: perf. of ἐμπίπλημι, "you have filled with" + gen.

εἴποιμι: aor. opt. pot., "*I could not say* it otherwise"

ὁπόταν ... ἀκούσῃ: aor. subj. in general temporal clause, "whenever someone hears"

General or Indefinite Clauses

Various kinds of subordinate clauses that are general or indefinite (if ever, whenever, whoever, etc.) use the subjunctive with ἂν in primary sequence, the optative without ἂν in secondary sequence:

ὁπόταν ταῦρος ᾖς "whenever you are a bull"

πᾶς βωμὸς χρησμῳδεῖ, ὃς ἂν ἐλαίῳ περιχυθῇ: "any altar *which is drenched* in oil gives an oracle"

ὥστε οὐδ' ἢν προπίῃ τις ξυνίησι: "and so he does not understand, *if (ever) someone toasts* him"

14

ὅτι ὁ Ἡρακλῆς μὲν θεὸς ἀπεδείχθη, ὁ δὲ Εὐρυσθεύς,
ὃς ἐπέταττεν αὐτῷ, τέθνηκεν, καὶ πλησίον Ἡρακλέους
νεὼς οἰκέτου ὄντος καὶ Εὐρυσθέως τάφος τοῦ δεσπότου
αὐτοῦ, καὶ πάλιν ἐν Θήβαις Διόνυσος μὲν θεός, οἱ δ᾽
ἀνεψιοὶ αὐτοῦ ὁ Πενθεὺς καὶ ὁ Ἀκταίων καὶ ὁ Λέαρχος
ἀνθρώπων ἁπάντων κακοδαιμονέστατοι.

Ἀφ᾽ οὗ δὲ ἅπαξ σύ, ὦ Ζεῦ, ἀνέῳξας τοῖς τοιούτοις τὰς
θύρας καὶ ἐπὶ τὰς θνητὰς ἐτράπου, ἅπαντες μεμίμηνταί
σε, καὶ οὐχ οἱ ἄρρενες μόνον, ἀλλ᾽, ὅπερ αἴσχιστον, καὶ

αἴσχιστος, -ή, -όν: most shameful
Ἀκταίων, ὁ: Actaeon
ἀνεψιός, ὁ: a first-cousin, cousin
ἀνοίγνυμι: to open
ἅπαξ: once
ἀποδείκνυμι: to display, appoint
ἄρσην, ὁ: male
δεσπότης, -ου, ὁ: a master
Διόνυσος, ὁ: Dionysus
ἐπιτάττω: to put upon, command
Εὐρυσθεύς, ὁ: Eurystheus
Ἡρακλέης, ὁ: Heracles
θεός, ὁ: a god
Θῆβαι, -ῶν, αἱ: Thebes

θνητός, -ή, -όν: mortal
θύρα, ἡ: a door
κακοδαίμων, -ον: unlucky, miserable
Λέαρχος, ὁ: Learchus
μιμέομαι: to mimic, imitate
νεώς, -ώ, ὁ: temple, sanctuary
οἰκέτης, -ου, ὁ: a house-slave, menial
πάλιν: again
Πενθεὺς, ὁ: Pentheus
πλησίον: near (+ gen.)
τάφος, ὁ: a tomb
τοιοῦτος, -αύτη, -οῦτο: such as this
τρέπω: to turn

ὅτι ... ἀπεδείχθη: aor. pass. in ind. st., "hears *that Heracles was appointed*"

ἐπέταττεν: impf., "who *used to command* him" Heracles was forced to serve
   Eurystheus by the conniving of Hera

τέθνηκεν: perf., "Eurystheus *has died*" i.e. is dead

οἰκέτου: pred. agreeing with Ἡρακλέους, "Heracles being *the servant*"

Διόνυσος μὲν ... οἱ δ᾽ ἀνεψιοὶ: "while Dionysus is a god ... his relatives are"

Πενθεὺς ... Ἀκταίων ... Λέαρχος: the mothers of these men were the sisters of Semele.
   Pentheus was killed by his own mother, Agave; Actaeon was transformed into a
   bear by Artemis; Learchus was killed by his father, Athamas

ἀφ᾽ οὗ (sc. χρόνῳ): "from the moment"

ἀνέῳξας: aor., "you once opened"

ἐτράπου: aor. mid. of τρέπω, "you turned your attention to"

μεμίμηνται: perf. of μιμέομαι, "all *have imitated* you"

καὶ οὐχ ... μόνον: "and not only"

ἀλλ᾽ ... καὶ: "but also"

αἱ θήλειαι θεοί. τίς γὰρ οὐκ οἶδεν τὸν Ἀγχίσην καὶ τὸν Τιθωνὸν καὶ τὸν Ἐνδυμίωνα καὶ τὸν Ἰασίωνα καὶ τοὺς ἄλλους; ὥστε ταῦτα μὲν ἐάσειν μοι δοκῶ: μακρὸν γὰρ ἂν τὸ διελέγχειν γένοιτο.

ΖΕΥΣ: Μηδὲν περὶ τοῦ Γανυμήδους, ὦ Μῶμε, εἴπῃς: χαλεπανῶ γὰρ εἰ λυπήσεις τὸ μειράκιον ὀνειδίσας ἐς τὸ γένος.

ΜΩΜΟΣ: Οὐκοῦν μηδὲ περὶ τοῦ ἀετοῦ εἴπω, ὅτι καὶ οὗτος ἐν τῷ οὐρανῷ ἐστιν, ἐπὶ τοῦ βασιλείου σκήπτρου καθεζόμενος καὶ μονονουχὶ ἐπὶ κεφαλήν σοι νεοττεύων,

---

Ἀγχίσης, ὁ: Anchises
ἀετός, -οῦ, ὁ: an eagle
βασίλειος, -α, -ον: royal
Γανυμήδης, ὁ; Ganymede
γένος, -ους, τό: race, stock, family
διελέγχω: to pass censure
Ἐνδυμίων, ὁ: Endymion
θῆλυς, -εια, -υ: female
Ἰασίων, ὁ: Iasion
καθέζομαι: to sit down on
κεφαλή, ἡ: the head

λυπέω: to grieve, vex, annoy
μακρός, -ά, -ον: long
μειράκιον, τό: a boy, lad
μονονουχὶ (=οὐ μόνον): nearly, all but
νεοττεύω: to nest on
ὀνειδίζω: to throw a reproach upon
οὐκοῦν: therefore, then, accordingly
οὐρανός, ὁ: heaven
σκῆπτρον, τό: a sceptre
Τιθωνός, ὁ: Tithonus
χαλεπαίνω: to be angry

Ἀγχίσην etc: all lovers of goddesses, Anchises of Aphrodite, Tithonus of Eos, Endymion of Selene, Iasion of Demeter.

ἐάσειν: fut. inf. after δοκῶ, "I think *I will allow* these" i.e. pass over them, an example of *praeteritio*

τὸ διελέγχειν: pres. inf. articular, "the censuring"

γένοιτο: aor. opt. pot. of γίγνομαι, "the censuring *would be* long"

Γανυμήδους: Ganymede was a mortal lover of Zeus

εἴπῃς: aor. subj. in prohibition, "say nothing!"

χαλεπανῶ γὰρ εἰ λυπήσεις: both verbs are future indicating a threatening tone, "*I shall be angry if you grieve* the boy"

ὀνειδίσας: aor. part. instrumental, "grieve *by disparaging*"

εἴπω: aor. subj. in rhetorical question introducing yet another *praeteritio*, "am I not to speak?"

καὶ οὗτος: "and that this one too" i.e. the eagle, the form Zeus took to ravish Ganymede

καθεζόμενος: "pres. part., "being seated" an eagle topped the scepter of Zeus and Momus suggests that it is the very eagle that ravished Ganymede

θεὸς εἶναι δοκῶν; ἢ καὶ τοῦτον τοῦ Γανυμήδους ἕνεκα
ἐάσομεν;

Ἀλλ' ὁ Ἄττης γε, ὦ Ζεῦ, καὶ ὁ Κορύβας καὶ ὁ
Σαβάζιος, πόθεν ἡμῖν ἐπεισεκυκλήθησαν οὗτοι, ἢ ὁ
Μίθρης ἐκεῖνος, ὁ Μῆδος, ὁ τὸν κάνδυν καὶ τὴν τιάραν,
οὐδὲ ἑλληνίζων τῇ φωνῇ, ὥστε οὐδ' ἢν προπίῃ τις ξυνίῃσι;
τοιγαροῦν οἱ Σκύθαι ταῦτα ὁρῶντες, οἱ Γέται αὐτῶν,
μακρὰ ἡμῖν χαίρειν εἰπόντες αὐτοὶ ἀπαθανατίζουσι
καὶ θεοὺς χειροτονοῦσιν οὓς ἂν ἐθελήσωσι, τὸν αὐτὸν

ἀπαθανατίζω: to aim at immortality	Μῆδος, ὁ: a Mede
Ἄττης, ὁ: Attis	Μίθρας, ὁ: Mithras
Γέται, οἱ: the Getae, a Thracian tribe	ξυνίημι: to understand
δοκέω: to seem	πόθεν: whence?
ἐθέλω: to will, wish, purpose	προπίνω: to toast
εἶπον: to speak, say (*aor.*)	Σαβάζιος, ὁ: Sabazius
ἑλληνίζω: to be Greek	Σκύθης, -ου, ὁ: a Scythian
ἕνεκα: because of (+ *gen.*)	τιάρα, -ου, ἡ: a tiara
ἐπεισκυκλέω: to bring in one upon another	τοιγαροῦν: therefore, accordingly
κάνδυς, -υος, ὁ: a Median cloak with sleeves	φωνή, ἡ: a language
Κορύβας, ὁ: a priest of Cybele in Phrygia	χαίρω: to rejoice, be glad, be delighted
μακρός, -ά, -ον: long	χειροτονέω: to extend

ἐάσομεν: fut., "*shall I pass over* this too"

Ἄττης: Momus now turns to various "eastern" deities. Attis was the consort of the
Phrygian goddess Cybele; his self-castration was a prominent feature of his story.

Κορύβας: The Corybantes are usually a group of ecstatic dancers devoted to Cybele

Σαβάζιος: a Thracian and Phrygian god identified both with Zeus and Dionysus

ἐπεισεκυκλήθησαν: aor. pass. of ἐπι-εἰσ-κυκλέω, "how *have these been piled in upon
us*?"

Μίθρης: a Persian deity whose cult spread in the Roman empire, albeit much revised

ἑλληνίζων: pres. part., "*being Hellenized* in language" i.e. learning Greek

ὥστε οὐδ' ... ξυνίῃσι: pres. in result clause, "so that he doesn't understand"

ἢν προπίῃ: pres. subj. of προ-πίνω, in present general protasis, "if someone toasts
him"

οἱ Γέται αὐτῶν: "the Getae among them" but the Getae are Thracians, not Scythians

εἰπόντες: aor. part., "*having said* farewell"

οὓς ἂν ἐθελήσωσι: aor. subj. in general relative clause, "whomever they wish"

τρόπον ὅνπερ καὶ Ζάμολξις δοῦλος ὢν παρενεγράφη
οὐκ οἶδ' ὅπως διαλαθών.

Καίτοι πάντα ταῦτα, ὦ θεοί, μέτρια. σὺ δέ, ὦ
κυνοπρόσωπε καὶ σινδόσιν ἐσταλμένε Αἰγύπτιε, τίς

Αἰγύπτιος, -α, -ον: Egyptian	μέτριος, -α, -ον: within measure
διαλανθάνω: to escape notice, deceive	παρεγγράφω: to enroll fraudulently
δοῦλος, ὁ: a slave	σινδών, -όνος, ὁ: a fine cloth
Ζάμολξις, ὁ: Zamolxis	στέλλω: to array, don
κυνοπρόσωπος, -ον: dog-faced	τρόπος, ὁ: a turn, manner

τὸν αὐτὸν τρόπον: acc. of manner, "in the same manner"

Ζάμολξις: Herodous IV, 94–96 reports that Zalmoxis preached immortality to his countrymen and hid in a cave for several years to fake a return from the dead, hence his "fraudulent enrollment" among the gods

ὤν: pres. part. concessive, "although being a slave"

παρενεγράφη: aor. pass. of παρα-ἐν-γράφω, "he was fraudulently enrolled"

οὐκ οἶδ' ὅπως: parenthetical, "I don't know how"

διαλαθών: aor. part. of δια-λανθάνω, "having deceived"

κυνοπρόσωπε: voc., "oh dog-face" i.e. Anubis, the Egyptian god of mumification

ἐσταλμένε: perf. part. mid. voc. of στέλλω, "O you who have donned" + acc.

Circumstantial Participles

Circumstantial participles are added to a noun or a pronoun to set forth some circumstance under which an action takes place. The circumstances can be of the following types: time, manner, means, cause, purpose, concession, condition or attendant circumstance. Although sometimes particles can specify the type of circumstance, often only the context can clarify its force. Here are some examples:

Time: θεοὶ δόξαντες ἐμπεπλήκασι μὲν τὸν οὐρανὸν: "*after having been deemed* to be gods, they have filled heaven"

Means: σύ, ὦ Ζεῦ, παρέσχες θνηταῖς ἐπιμιγνύμενος: "you, Zeus, provided the beginning *by mingling* with mortals."

Concession: Ζάμολξις δοῦλος ὢν παρενεγράφη: Zamolxis, *although being* a slave, was fraudulently enrolled."

Cause: Μηκέτι τονθορύζετε, ὦ θεοί ... ἀγανακτοῦντες: "Don't grumble, Gods ... *because you are annoyed.*

Manner: Ζάμολξις δοῦλος ὢν παρενεγράφη ... διαλαθών: "Zamolxis, although being a slave, was fraudulently enrolled *having escaped our notice.* (i.e. secretly)"

Attendant Circumstance: μετέχουσιν, οὐδὲ καταβαλόντες ἡμῖν τὸ μετοίκιον: "They have a share, not even *having paid* the metic tax."

The circumstantial participle can also stand in the genitive absolute construction: ἐκκλησίας ἐννόμου ἀγομένης: "a regular assembly *being convened*"

εἶ, ὦ βέλτιστε, ἢ πῶς ἀξιοῖς θεὸς εἶναι ὑλακτῶν; τί δὲ
βουλόμενος καὶ ὁ ποικίλος οὗτος ταῦρος ὁ Μεμφίτης
προσκυνεῖται καὶ χρᾷ καὶ προφήτας ἔχει; αἰσχύνομαι γὰρ
ἴβιδας καὶ πιθήκους εἰπεῖν καὶ τράγους καὶ ἄλλα πολλῷ
γελοιότερα οὐκ οἶδ' ὅπως ἐξ Αἰγύπτου παραβυσθέντα ἐς
τὸν οὐρανόν, ἃ ὑμεῖς, ὦ θεοί, πῶς ἀνέχεσθε ὁρῶντες ἐπ'

Αἴγυπτος, ὁ: Egypt	οὐρανός, ὁ: heaven
αἰσχύνομαι: to be ashamed	παραβύω: to stuff in, insert
ἀνέχω: to hold up, endure	πίθηκος, ὁ: an ape, monkey
ἀξιόω: to deem worthy, seek to	ποικίλος, -η, -ον: dappled
βέλτιστος, -η, -ον: best	προσκυνέω: to worship
βούλομαι: to will, wish, be willing	προφήτης, -ου, ὁ: a prophet
γέλοιος, -α, -ον: laughable	ταῦρος, ὁ: a bull
ἴβις, -δος, ὁ: an ibis	τράγος, ὁ: a he-goat
Μεμφίτης, ὁ: a Memphite	ὑλακτέω: to bark, bay, howl
ὁράω: to see	χράω: to declare oracles

ὦ βέλτιστε: "O best one" ironic

ἀξιοῖς: pres., "how do you seek to?" + inf.

ὑλακτῶν: pres. inf. of attendant circumstance, "with your barking"

τί δὲ βουλόμενος: "wishing what?" i.e. why?

ταῦρος: the Apis bull, which was a manifestation of the Memphite god Ptah, and a
frequent object of ridicule by Greeks

προσκυνεῖται: pres. pass., "why *is he worshipped*"

ἴβιδας καὶ πιθήκους: the ibis was a bird sacred to Egyptian Thoth, who was often
depicted with the head of an ibis and sometimes with the head of baboon

τράγους: a goat-headed deity worshipped at Mendes in the Nile delta region is
mentioned by Herodotus 2.42, 46 and 166

πολλῷ: dat. of degree of difference, "more laughable *by much*"

οὐκ οἶδ' ὅπως: parenthetical, "I don't know how"

παραβυσθέντα: aor. part. pass. of παραβύω, "*having been inserted* into heaven" i.e.
smuggled in

ὁρῶντες: pres. part. supplementing ἀνέχεσθε, "how do you endure *seeing*"

ἴσης ἢ καὶ μᾶλλον ὑμῶν προσκυνούμενα; ἢ σύ, ὦ Ζεῦ, πῶς φέρεις ἐπειδὰν κριοῦ κέρατα φύσωσί σοι;

ΖΕΥΣ: Αἰσχρὰ ὡς ἀληθῶς ταῦτα φῂς τὰ περὶ τῶν Αἰγυπτίων· ὅμως δ' οὖν, ὦ Μῶμε, τὰ πολλὰ αὐτῶν αἰνίγματά ἐστιν, καὶ οὐ πάνυ χρὴ καταγελᾶν ἀμύητον ὄντα.

ΜΩΜΟΣ: Πάνυ γοῦν μυστηρίων, ὦ Ζεῦ, δεῖ ἡμῖν, ὡς εἰδέναι θεοὺς μὲν τοὺς θεούς, κυνοκεφάλους δὲ τοὺς κυνοκεφάλους.

ΖΕΥΣ: Ἔα, φημί, τὰ περὶ Αἰγυπτίων· ἄλλοτε γὰρ περὶ τούτων ἐπισκεψόμεθα ἐπὶ σχολῆς. σὺ δὲ τοὺς ἄλλους λέγε.

Αἰγύπτιος, -α, -ον: Egyptian
αἴνιγμα, -ατος, τό: a riddle, mystery
αἰσχρός, -ά, -όν: causing shame
ἀληθῶς: truly
ἄλλοτε: at another time, at other times
ἀμύητος, -ον: uninitiated
γοῦν: at least then, at any rate, any way
δεῖ: to be necessary
ἐπισκέπτομαι: to look carefully at (+ gen.)
ἴσος, -η, -ον: equal to
καταγελάω: to jeer or mock

κέρας, -ατος, τό: the horn of an animal
κριός, ὁ: a ram
κυνοκέφαλος, -ον: dog-headed
μυστήριον, τό: a mystery or secret doctrine
πάνυ: altogether, entirely
προσκυνέω: to worship
σχολή, ἡ: leisure
φέρω: to bear
φύω: to bring forth, produce, put forth
χρή: it is necessary

ὑμῶν: gen. of comparison, "or more *than you*"

προσκυνούμενα: pres. part. pass. in ind. st. after ὁρῶντες, "seeing *that they are being worshipped*"

ἐπειδὰν ... φύσωσι: aor. subj. in general temporal clause, "whenever they cause to grow"

κριοῦ κέρατα: "ram's horns" with which Zeus-Ammon was represented

ἀμύητον ὄντα: acc. subj. of καταγελᾶν, "for *one who is uninitiated* to laugh"

μυστηρίων: gen. after δεῖ, "great need there is *of mysteries*!" ironic

ὡς εἰδέναι: perf. inf. in result clause, "so that we know"

ΜΩΜΟΣ: Τὸν Τροφώνιον, ὦ Ζεῦ, καὶ ὃ μάλιστά με
ἀποπνίγει, τὸν Ἀμφίλοχον, ὃς ἐναγοῦς ἀνθρώπου καὶ
μητρολῴου υἱὸς ὢν μαντεύεται ὁ γενναῖος ἐν Κιλικίᾳ,
ψευδόμενος τὰ πολλὰ καὶ γοητεύων τοῖν δυοῖν ὀβολοῖν
ἕνεκα. τοιγαροῦν οὐκέτι σύ, ὦ Ἄπολλον, εὐδοκιμεῖς,
ἀλλὰ ἤδη πᾶς λίθος καὶ πᾶς βωμὸς χρησμῳδεῖ, ὃς ἂν
ἐλαίῳ περιχυθῇ καὶ στεφάνους ἔχῃ καὶ γόητος ἀνδρὸς
εὐπορήσῃ, οἷοι πολλοί εἰσιν. ἤδη καὶ ὁ Πολυδάμαντος τοῦ
ἀθλητοῦ ἀνδριὰς ἰᾶται τοὺς πυρέττοντας ἐν Ὀλυμπίᾳ

ἀθλητής: a prizefighter	Κιλίκια: Cilicia
ἀνδριάς, -άντος, ὁ: a statue	λίθος, ὁ: a stone
Ἀπόλλων, -ωνος, ὁ: Apollo	μαντεύομαι: to divine, prophesy
ἀποπνίγω: to choke, throttle	μητρολῴος, ου, ὁ: a matricide
βωμός, ὁ: an altar	ὀβολός, ὁ: an obol
γενναῖος, -α, -ον: suitable to one's birth	οἷος, -α, -ον: what sort or manner
γόης, -ητος, ὁ: a sorcerer, enchanter	Ὀλυμπία, ἡ: Olympia
γοητεύω: to bewitch, beguile	περιχέω: to pour round or over
ἔλαιον, τό: olive-oil	Πολυδάμας, -αντος, ὁ; Polydamas
ἐναγής, -ές: under a curse, outcast	πυρέττω: to be ill of a fever
ἕνεκα: on account of	στέφανος, ὁ: a garland
εὐδοκιμέω: to be honoured	τοιγαροῦν: therefore, accordingly
εὐπορέω, -ήσω: to prosper, thrive	υἱός, ὁ: a son
ἤδη: already	χρησμῳδέω: to chant oracles
ἰάομαι: to heal, cure	ψεύδομαι: to lie

Τροφώνιον: Trophonius, whose "cave" in Boeotia was a famous oracle, appears with
  Amphilochus in *DMort*. 3 (10)

Ἀμφίλοχον: Amphilochus, the son of Amphiarus, was an Argive hero who founded
  many oracles

ἐναγοῦς ... μητρολῴου: the "outcast" and "matricide" is Alcmaeon, the brother of
  Amphilochus; but Alcmaeon is the father of a second Amphilochus as well

ὢν: pres. part. concessive, "who, *although being* the son"

ὁ γενναῖος: "true to his birth" here ironic, "the miscreant"

τοῖν δυοῖν ὀβολοῖν: gen. dual after ἕνεκα, "for the sake *of two obols*"

ὃς ἂν ... περιχυθῇ: aor. subj. pass. of περι-χέω in general relative clause, "any altar
  which is drenched"

ἔχῃ ... εὐπορήσῃ: subj. also in general relative clauses, "which possesses ... which
  becomes furnished with" + gen.

Πολυδάμαντος: the statue of the famous champion Polydamas is mentioned by
  Pausanias (6.5.1)

καὶ ὁ Θεαγένους ἐν Θάσῳ, καὶ Ἕκτορι θύουσιν ἐν Ἰλίῳ καὶ Πρωτεσιλάῳ καταντικρὺ ἐν Χερρονήσῳ. ἀφ' οὗ δ' οὖν τοσοῦτοι γεγόναμεν, ἐπιδέδωκε μᾶλλον ἡ ἐπιορκία καὶ ἱεροσυλία, καὶ ὅλως καταπεφρονήκασιν ἡμῶν -- εὖ ποιοῦντες.

Καὶ ταῦτα μὲν περὶ τῶν νόθων καὶ παρεγγράπτων. ἐγὼ δὲ καὶ ξένα ὀνόματα πολλὰ ἤδη ἀκούων οὔτε ὄντων τινῶν παρ' ἡμῖν οὔτε συστῆναι ὅλως δυναμένων, πάνυ, ὦ Ζεῦ, καὶ ἐπὶ τούτοις γελῶ. ἢ ποῦ γάρ ἐστιν ἡ

ἀκούω: to hear
γελάω: to laugh
δύναμαι: to be able
Ἕκτωρ, -ορος, ὁ; Hector, the Trojan hero
ἐπιδίδωμι: to give besides, increase
ἐπιορκία, ἡ: a false oath
Θάσος, ὁ: the island of Thasos
Θεαγένους, ὁ: Theagenes
θύω: to sacrifice to (+ dat.)
ἱεροσυλία: a sacrilege
Ἴλιος ὁ: Troy

καταντικρύ: on the opposite side
καταφρονέω: to despise
νόθος, -η, -ον: bastard
ξένος, -η, -ον: foreign
ὅλως: entirely
ὄνομα, τό: name
παρέγγραπτος, -ον: illegally registered
Πρωτεσίλαος, ὁ: Protesilaus, whose hero cult was prominent in imperial times
συνίστημι: to set together
τοσοῦτος, -αύτη, -οῦτο: so large, so tall
Χερρονήσος, ὁ: the Chersonese or peninsula

Θεαγένους: the miraculous power of the statue of Theagenes, another Olympic champion, is reported by Pausanias (6.11.6-9)

Πρωτεσιλάῳ: the cult of the hero Protesilaus on the Thracian Chersonese is mentioned in several sources

ἀφ' οὗ (sc. χρόνῳ): "from which time"

γεγόναμεν: perf. of γίγνομαι, "*we have become* so numerous"

ἐπιδέδωκε: perf., "have increased"

μᾶλλον: "more and more"

καταπεφρονήκασιν: perf., "*they have come to despise* us"

εὖ ποιοῦντες: pres. part., "doing well" i.e. and so they should

οὔτε ὄντων ... δυναμένων: pres. part. gen. agreeing with τινῶν, "names of certain ones *neither existing ... nor being able to*" + inf.

συστῆναι: aor. inf. of συν-ίστημι after δυναμένων, "able *to exist*"

ἢ ποῦ γάρ: "for where indeed?"

πολυθρύλητος ἀρετὴ καὶ φύσις καὶ εἱμαρμένη καὶ τύχη,
ἀνυπόστατα καὶ κενὰ πραγμάτων ὀνόματα ὑπὸ βλακῶν
ἀνθρώπων τῶν φιλοσόφων ἐπινοηθέντα; καὶ ὅμως
αὐτοσχέδια ὄντα οὕτω τοὺς ἀνοήτους πέπεικεν, ὥστε
οὐδεὶς ἡμῖν οὐδὲ θύειν βούλεται, εἰδὼς ὅτι, κἂν μυρίας
ἑκατόμβας παραστήσῃ, ὅμως τὴν τύχην πράξουσαν τὰ

ἀνόητος, -ον: ignorant	μυρίος, -ος, -ον: numberless
ἀνυπόστατος, -ον: irresistible	ὄνομα, τό: a name
ἀρετή, ἡ: goodness, excellence	παρίστημι: to make to stand
αὐτοσχέδιος, -ον: improvised	πείθω: to persuade
βλάξ, -κος, ὁ: a stupid person	πολυθρύλητος, -ον: well known
βούλομαι: to will, wish	πρᾶγμα, -ατος, τό: a matter, business
εἱμαρμένη, ἡ: necessity	πράττω: to do, effect
ἑκατόμβη, ἡ: an offering of a hundred oxen	τύχη, ἡ: fortune
ἐπινοέω: to contrive, invent	φιλόσοφος, ὁ: a lover of wisdom
θύω: to sacrifice	φύσις, ἡ: nature
κενός, -ή, -όν: empty	

ἀρετὴ καὶ φύσις: "Virtue and Nature etc.," all equated with divine principles in
   various philosophies

ἐπινοηθέντα: aor. part. pass., "having been invented"

πέπεικεν: perf. of πείθω, "they have so persuaded"

ὥστε ... βούλεται: indic. in result clause emphasizing actual result, "so that no one
   wishes" + inf.

εἰδὼς: perf. part. in οἶδα agreeing with οὐδεὶς, "no one wishes, *since they know*"

κἂν ... παραστήσῃ: aor. subj. of παρα-ΐστημι in future more vivid protasis, "*even if
   they dedicate* sacrifices"

πράξουσαν: fut. part. in ind. st. after εἰδὼς, "since they know *that Chance will effect*"

Result Clauses

ὥστε (sometimes ὡς) introduces result clauses either with an infinitive or with a
finite verb.

ὥστε + infinitive indicates a possible or intended result, without emphasizing its
actual occurrence. The infinitive does not express time, but only aspect.

> ἐπιλέλοιπε δὲ ἡ ἀμβροσία καὶ τὸ νέκταρ, <u>ὥστε</u> μνᾶς ἤδη τὴν κοτύλην
> <u>εἶναι</u>: "The ambrosia and nectar has run low *so that* now a cup *costs* one
> mina."

ὥστε + indicative emphasizes the actual occurrence of the result. Both time and
aspect are indicated by the form of the verb.

> οὕτω τοὺς ἀνοήτους πέπεικεν, <u>ὥστε</u> οὐδεὶς ἡμῖν οὐδὲ θύειν <u>βούλεται</u>:
> "They have so persuaded the ignorant *that* no one *wishes* to sacrifice to us"

μεμοιραμένα καὶ ἃ ἐξ ἀρχῆς ἑκάστῳ ἐπεκλώσθη. ἡδέως
ἂν οὖν ἐροίμην σε, ὦ Ζεῦ, εἴ που εἶδες ἢ ἀρετὴν ἢ φύσιν
ἢ εἱμαρμένην; ὅτι μὲν γὰρ ἀεὶ καὶ σὺ ἀκούεις ἐν ταῖς τῶν
φιλοσόφων διατριβαῖς, οἶδα, εἰ μὴ καὶ κωφός τις εἶ, ὡς
βοώντων αὐτῶν μὴ ἐπαΐειν.

ἀεί: always, for ever
ἀκούω: to hear
ἀρετή, ἡ: goodness, excellence
ἀρχή, ἡ: a beginning
βοάω: to cry aloud, to shout
διατριβή, ἡ: a diatribe, sermon
εἱμαρμένη, ἡ: necessity
ἕκαστος, -η, -ον: each, each one

ἐπαίω: to listen to, hear
ἐπικλώθω: to spin (a thread)
ἐρωτάω: to ask, enquire
ἡδέως: sweetly
κωφός, -ή, -όν: blunt, dull, obtuse
μοιράω: to distribute, allocate
φιλόσοφος, ὁ: a lover of wisdom
φύσις, ἡ: nature

τὰ μεμοιραμένα: perf. part., "the things fated"
ἃ ... ἐπεκλώσθη: aor. pass., "what has been spun out" i.e. determined by Fate
ἂν οὖν ἐροίμην: aor. opt. pot., "so I would like to ask"
εἴ που εἶδες: ind. question, "ask *whether you know*"
ὡς ... μὴ ἐπαΐειν: inf. in result clause, "so that you do not hear" + gen.

Participles: General Principles

Participles fall into three broad classes of use, with many other distinctions:

1. Attributive participles modify a noun or pronoun like other adjectives. They can occur with an article in the attributive position or with no article:

πλείους γὰρ οἶδ' ὅτι ἔσονται οἱ μὴ χειροτονήσοντες: "for I know that *those who will not raise their hands* will be more numerous."

2. Circumstantial participles are added to a noun or pronoun to set forth some circumstance under which an action takes place. Although agreeing with a noun or pronoun, these participles actually qualify the verb in a sentence, indicating time, manner, means, cause, purpose, concession, condition or attendant circumstance. Circumstantial participles can occur in the genitive absolute construction.

οὐδὲν ὑποστειλάμενος ἐρῶ: "I will speak, *having held back* not at all."
For more examples, see p. 18

3. Supplementary participles complete the idea of certain verbs. Often it is the participle itself that expresses the main action:

πῶς ἀνέχεσθε ὁρῶντες: "How do you endure *seeing* them"
The participial form of indirect discourse after verbs of showing and perceiving is a special class of supplementary participles.

ὁρῶ γοῦν πολλοὺς ἀχθομένους: "I see that many *are becoming annoyed*"

Πολλὰ ἔτι ἔχων εἰπεῖν καταπαύσω τὸν λόγον· ὁρῶ
γοῦν πολλοὺς ἀχθομένους μοι λέγοντι καὶ συρίττοντας,
ἐκείνους μάλιστα ὧν καθήψατο ἡ παρρησία τῶν λόγων.
πέρας γοῦν, εἰ ἐθέλεις, ὦ Ζεῦ, ψήφισμά τι περὶ τούτων
ἀναγνώσομαι ἤδη ξυγγεγραμμένον.

ΖΕΥΣ: Ἀνάγνωθι· οὐ πάντα γὰρ ἀλόγως ἠτιάσω. καὶ δεῖ τὰ
πολλὰ αὐτῶν ἐπισχεῖν, ὡς μὴ ἐπὶ πλεῖον ἂν γίγνηται.

αἰτιάομαι: to charge, accuse
ἄλογος, -ον: without reason
ἀναγιγνώσκω: to read out
ἄχθομαι: to be loaded
γοῦν: at least then, at any rate, any way
δεῖ: to be necessary
ἐθέλω: to will, wish, purpose
καθάπτω: to fasten, fix or put upon

καταπαύω: to lay to rest, put an end to
ξυγγράφω: to write or note down
ὁράω: to see
παρρησία, ἡ: freespokenness
πέρας, -ατος, τό: an end, limit
πλείων, πλεῖον: more
συρίττω: to whisper
ψήφισμα, -ατος, τό: a proposal, decree

ἀχθομένους ... συρίττοντας: pres. part. in ind. st. after ὁρῶ, "I see that many *are
becoming annoyed and are whispering*"
καθήψατο: aor. mid. of κατα-ἅπτω, "my frankness *has fixed upon*" + gen.
πέρας: acc. adverbial, "in conclusion"
ἀναγνώσομαι: fut., "I will read out"
ξυγγεγραμμένον: perf. part. of ξυν-γράφω, "something already *composed*"
ἀνάγνωθι: aor. imper. of ἀνα-γιγνώσκω, "read out!"
ἠτιάσω: aor. 2 sing. mid., "you accused"
ὡς μὴ ... ἂν γίγνηται: pres. subj. in neg. purpose clause, "lest they become"
ἐπὶ πλεῖον: "more so"

ΜΩΜΟΣ: Ἀγαθῇ τύχῃ. Ἐκκλησίας ἐννόμου ἀγομένης ἑβδόμῃ ἱσταμένου ὁ Ζεὺς ἐπρυτάνευε καὶ προήδρευε Ποσειδῶν, ἐπεστάτει Ἀπόλλων, ἐγραμμάτευε Μῶμος Νυκτὸς καὶ ὁ Ὕπνος τὴν γνώμην εἶπεν. Ἐπειδὴ πολλοὶ τῶν ξένων, οὐ μόνον Ἕλληνες ἀλλὰ καὶ βάρβαροι, οὐδαμῶς ἄξιοι ὄντες κοινωνεῖν ἡμῖν τῆς πολιτείας, παρεγγραφέντες οὐκ οἶδα ὅπως καὶ θεοὶ δόξαντες ἐμπεπλήκασι μὲν τὸν οὐρανὸν ὡς μεστὸν εἶναι τὸ συμπόσιον ὄχλου ταραχώδους

ἄγω: to lead	μεστός, -ή, -όν: full
ἄξιος, -ία, -ον: worthy	ξένος, ὁ: a foreigner
βάρβαρος, ὁ: a barbarian	οὐδαμῶς: in no wise
γνώμη, ἡ: a resolution	οὐρανός, ὁ: heaven
γραμματεύω: to be secretary	ὄχλος, ὁ: a throng, mob
δοκέω: to seem, to be considered	παρεγγράφω: to enroll illegally
ἕβδομος, -η, -ον: seventh	πολιτεία, ἡ: citizenship
ἐκκλησία, ἡ: an assembly	προεδρεύω: to act as president
Ἕλλην, -ηνος, ὁ: a Greek	πρυτανεύω: to serve as a member of the
ἐμπίμπλημι: to fill	executive committee
ἔννομος, -ον: lawful, legal	συμπόσιον, τό: a symposium
ἐπιστατέω: to serve as chairman	ταραχώδης, -ες: disturbing
ἵστημι: to make to stand	τύχη, ἡ: fortune
κοινωνέω: to share of or take part in	ὕπνος, ὁ: sleep

ἀγαθῇ τύχῃ: dat. in a common formula like many of the following phrases, "may there be good fortune"

ἐκκλησίας ... ἀγομένης: gen. abs., "a regular assembly being convened"

ἑβδόμῃ (sc. ἡμέρᾳ): "held *on the seventh* day"

ἱσταμένου: pres. part. pass. agreeing with ἐκκλησίας, "being established"

ἐπρυτάνευε ... προήδρευε ... ἐπεστάτει ... ἐγραμμάτευε: impf. referring to the offices of the *prytaneis* (executive committee of the assembly), *proedros* (president of the executive committee), *epistates* (chairman of the executive committee) and *grammateus* (secretary)

Νυκτὸς (sc. υἱὸς): "son *of Night*"

τὴν γνώμην εἶπεν" Sleep *made the resolution*"

κοινωνεῖν: inf. epexegetic after ἄξιοι, "worthy *to share in*" + gen.

παρεγγραφέντες: aor. part. pass. of παρα-εν-γράφω, "having been enrolled illegally"

οὐκ οἶδα ὅπως: parenthetical, "I don't know how"

θεοὶ: nom. pred., "having been considered *gods*"

ἐμπεπλήκασι: perf. of ἐν-πίμπλημι, "they have filled"

ὡς ... εἶναι: inf. in result clause, "*so that the symposium is* full of" + gen.

ταραχώδους: gen. agreeing with ὄχλου, "full of a *disturbing* crowd"

πολυγλώσσων τινῶν καὶ ξυγκλύδων ἀνθρώπων,
ἐπιλέλοιπε δὲ ἡ ἀμβροσία καὶ τὸ νέκταρ, ὥστε μνᾶς
ἤδη τὴν κοτύλην εἶναι διὰ τὸ πλῆθος τῶν πινόντων· οἱ
δὲ ὑπὸ αὐθαδείας παρωσάμενοι τοὺς παλαιούς τε καὶ
ἀληθεῖς θεοὺς προεδρίας ἠξιώκασιν αὐτοὺς παρὰ πάντα
τὰ πάτρια καὶ ἐν τῇ γῇ προτιμᾶσθαι θέλουσι· Δεδόχθαι
τῇ βουλῇ καὶ τῷ δήμῳ ξυλλεγῆναι μὲν ἐκκλησίαν ἐν τῷ
Ὀλύμπῳ περὶ τροπὰς χειμερινάς, ἑλέσθαι δὲ ἐπιγνώμονας

αἱρέομαι: to choose, elect
ἀληθής, -ές: unconcealed, true
ἀμβροσία, ἡ: ambrosia
ἀξιόω: to think worthy of
αὐθάδεια: wilfulness, presumption
βουλή, ἡ: executive committee
γῆ, ἡ: earth
δῆμος, ὁ: the people
ἐκκλησία, ἡ: an assembly
ἐπιγνώμων, -ονος, ὁ: an arbiter
ἐπιλείπω: to leave behind, run low
θέλω: to will, wish, purpose
κοτύλη, ἡ: a cup
μνᾶ, ἡ: a mna (a measure)

νέκταρ, -αρος, τό: nectar
ξύγκλυς, -υδος, ὁ: promiscuous
ξυλλέγω: to gather
Ὄλυμπος, ὁ: Olympus
παλαιός, -ά, -όν: old in years
παρωθέω: to push aside X (*acc.*) from Y (*gen.*)
πάτριος, -α, -ον: of one's father, traditional
πίνω: to drink
πλῆθος, -εος, τό: a multitude
πολύγλωσσος, -ον: many-tongued
προεδρία, ἡ: the privilege of the front seats
προτιμάω: to honour
τροπή, ἡ: a turn (of the sun's course), solstice
χειμερινός, -ή, -όν: of winter

ἐπιλέλοιπε: perf., "the ambrosia *has run low*"

ὥστε ... εἶναι: result clause, "*so that* a cup *is*"

μνᾶς: gen. of price, "costs a *mna*"

τῶν πινόντων: pres. part. gen. partitive, "number *of those drinking*"

ὑπὸ αὐθαδείας: the agency expression, "by their boldness"

παρωσάμενοι: aor. part. of παρα-ωθέω, "having pushed aside"

ἠξιώκασιν: perf., "*they have deemed* themselves *worthy*"

αὑτοὺς (=ἑαυτοὺς): reflexive, "deemed *themselves*"

προτιμᾶσθαι: pres. inf. pass. complementing θέλουσι, "wish *to be honored*"

δεδόχθαι: perf. inf. pass. of δοκέω used as an imperative, "be it resolved!" and governing the infinitives in the next several sentences

ξυλλεγῆναι: aor. inf. pass. of ξυν-λέγω after δεδόχθαι, "resolved that the assembly *be gathered*"

περὶ τροπὰς χειμερινάς: "in the winter solstice"

ἑλέσθαι: aor. inf. of αἱρέομαι, also after δεδόχθαι, "resolved *to choose*"

ἐπιγνώμονας: acc. pred., "choose *as arbiters*"

τελείους θεοὺς ἑπτά, τρεῖς μὲν ἐκ τῆς παλαιᾶς βουλῆς
τῆς ἐπὶ Κρόνου, τέτταρας δὲ ἐκ τῶν δώδεκα, καὶ ἐν
αὐτοῖς τὸν Δία· τούτους δὲ τοὺς ἐπιγνώμονας αὐτοὺς
μὲν καθέζεσθαι ὀμόσαντας τὸν νόμιμον ὅρκον τὴν
Στύγα, τὸν Ἑρμῆν δὲ κηρύξαντα ξυναγαγεῖν ἅπαντας
ὅσοι ἀξιοῦσι ξυντελεῖν ἐς τὸ ξυνέδριον, τοὺς δὲ ἥκειν
μάρτυρας ἐπαγομένους ἐνωμότους καὶ ἀποδείξεις τοῦ
γένους. τοὐντεῦθεν δὲ οἱ μὲν παρίτωσαν καθ’ ἕνα, οἱ δὲ
ἐπιγνώμονες ἐξετάζοντες ἢ θεοὺς εἶναι ἀποφανοῦνται ἢ

ἀξιόω: to demand
ἀπόδειξις, -εως, ἡ: a proof
ἀποφαίνω: to show fort, display
βουλή, ἡ: executive committee
γένος, -ους, τό: race, stock, family
δώδεκα: twelve
εἷς, μία, ἕν: one
ἐντεῦθεν: hence or thence
ἐνώμοτος, -ον: bound by oath
ἐξετάζω: to examine closely
ἐπάγω: to bring on
ἐπιγνώμων, -ονος, ὁ: an arbiter
ἑπτά: seven
Ἑρμῆς, -οῦ, ὁ: Hermes
ἥκω: to have come, be present
καθέζομαι: to sit down

κηρύττω: to proclaim officially
Κρόνος, ὁ: Cronus
μάρτυς, -υρος, ὁ: a witness
νόμιμος, -η, -ον: legal
ξυνάγω: to bring together, convene
ξυνέδριον, τό: a council
ξυντελέω: to accomplish
ὄμνυμι: to swear
ὅρκος, ὁ: the witness of an oath
παλαιός, -ά, -όν: old in years
παρέρχομαι” to advance
Στύξ, ἡ: the Styx
τέλειος, -α, -ον: finished, perfect
τέτταρες, -ων, οἱ: four
τρεῖς, τρία: three

τῆς ἐπὶ Κρόνου: "the committee *from Cronus' time*"
ἐκ τῶν δώδεκα: "from the twelve (Olympians)"
καθέζεσθαι: pres. inf., "(resolved) that these sit down" i.e. meet
ὀμόσαντας: aor. part. agreeing with τούτους, "these, *having sworn*"
τὴν Στύγα: swearing by the Styx was the most serious divine oath
κηρύξαντα: aor. part. instrumental, "that Hermes, *by having proclaimed*"
ξυναγαγεῖν: aor. inf., "(resolved) that Hermes *convene*"
ξυντελεῖν: fut. inf. after ἀξιοῦσι, "whoever demands *to make pay the tax*" i.e. to be
  counted among our community, since paying taxes is the basis for inclusion
τοὺς δὲ: "*and that these* come"
ἐπαγομένους: pres. part. acc., "*bringing* witnesses"
ἀποδείξεις: acc., "demonstrations" i.e. documentation
οἱ μὲν παρίτωσαν: pres. imper. 3 pl. of παρα-έρχομαι, "let them advance"
ἀποφανοῦνται: fut., "these will show forth"

28

καταπέμψουσιν ἐπὶ τὰ σφέτερα ἠρία καὶ τὰς θήκας τὰς
προγονικάς. ἢν δέ τις ἁλῷ τῶν ἀδοκίμων καὶ ἅπαξ ὑπὸ
τῶν ἐπιγνωμόνων ἐκκριθέντων ἐπιβαίνων τοῦ οὐρανοῦ,
ἐς τὸν Τάρταρον ἐμπεσεῖν τοῦτον. Ἐργάζεσθαι δὲ τὰ
αὐτοῦ ἕκαστον, καὶ μήτε τὴν Ἀθηνᾶν ἰᾶσθαι μήτε τὸν
Ἀσκληπιὸν χρησμῳδεῖν μήτε τὸν Ἀπόλλω τοσαῦτα
μόνον ποιεῖν, ἀλλὰ ἕν τι ἐπιλεξάμενον μάντιν ἢ
κιθαρῳδὸν ἢ ἰατρὸν εἶναι. τοῖς δὲ φιλοσόφοις προειπεῖν

ἀδόκιμος, -ον: spurious
Ἀθήνη, ἡ: Athena, goddess of crafts
ἁλίσκομαι: to be taken, conquered
ἅπαξ: once
Ἀπόλλων, -ωνος, -ω, ὁ: god of healing,
    prophecy and music
Ἀσκληπιός, ὁ: god of healing
εἷς, μία, ἕν: one
ἕκαστος, -η, -ον: each
ἐκκρίνω: to choose
ἐμπίπτω: fall upon
ἐπιβαίνω: to go upon, enter
ἐπιγνώμων, -ονος, ὁ: an arbiter
ἐπιλέγω: to choose, pick out, select
ἐργάζομαι: to work, accomplish
ἠρίον, τό: a mound, tomb

θήκη, ἡ: a box, chest
ἰάομαι: to heal, cure
ἰατρός, ὁ: a physician
καταπέμπω: to send down
κιθαρῳδός, ὁ: a harper
μάντις, -εως, ὁ: a seer, prophet
μόνον: only, alone
οὐρανός, ὁ: heaven
προγονικός, -ή, -όν: parental
προεῖπον: to tell or state before
σφέτερος, -α, -ον: their own, their
Τάρταρος, ὁ: Tartarus
τοσοῦτος, -αύτη, -οῦτο: so many
φιλόσοφος, ὁ: a lover of wisdom
χρησμῳδέω: to chant oracles

καταπέμψουσιν: fut., "or they will send away"

ἢν δέ τις ἁλῷ: aor. subj. of **ἁλίσκομαι** in present general protasis, "if anyone is
    caught" + part.

τῶν ... ἐκκριθέντων: aor. part. pass. gen. pl. partitive with **τις**, "if anyone *of those
    having been judged*"

ἀδοκίμων: gen. pred., "judged (to be) *illegal*"

ἐπιβαίνων: pres. part. after **ἁλῷ**, "is caught *entering*" + gen.

ἐμπεσεῖν: aor. inf. also governed by **δεδόχθαι**, "resolved *that he fall*"

τὰ αὐτοῦ: "each accomplish *his own things*"

μήτε ... ἰᾶσθαι: "(resolved) that Athena *not heal*"

μήτε ... χρησμῳδεῖν: "that Asclepius *not prophesize*"

μήτε ... ποιεῖν: "that Apollo alone *not do*"

ἐπιλεξάμενον: aor. part. agreeing with **Ἀπόλλω**, "*having chosen* one"

προειπεῖν: aor. inf., "(resolved) to warn"

μὴ ἀναπλάττειν κενὰ ὀνόματα μηδὲ ληρεῖν περὶ ὧν
οὐκ ἴσασιν. ὁπόσοι δὲ ἤδη ναῶν ἢ θυσιῶν ἠξιώθησαν,
ἐκείνων μὲν καθαιρεθῆναι τὰ ἀγάλματα, ἐντεθῆναι δὲ ἢ
Διὸς ἢ Ἥρας ἢ Ἀπόλλωνος ἢ τῶν ἄλλων τινός, ἐκείνοις
δὲ τάφον χῶσαι τὴν πόλιν καὶ στήλην ἐπιστῆσαι ἀντὶ
βωμοῦ. ἢν δέ τις παρακούσῃ τοῦ κηρύγματος καὶ μὴ
ἐθελήσῃ ἐπὶ τοὺς ἐπιγνώμονας ἐλθεῖν, ἐρήμην αὐτοῦ
καταδιαιτησάτωσαν. Τοῦτο μὲν ὑμῖν τὸ ψήφισμα.

ἄγαλμα, -ατος, τό: a statue
ἀναπλάττω: to remodel, fashion
ἀξιόω: to think worthy of
βωμός, ὁ: an altar
ἐθέλω: to will, wish
ἐντίθημι: to put in or into
ἐπιγνώμων, -ονος, ὁ: an arbiter
ἐρήμη, ἡ: a judgement by default
ἐφίστημι: to set or place upon
θυσία, ἡ: an offering
καθαιρέω: to take down
καταδιαιτάω: to give a judgement against X (gen.)

κενός, -ή, -όν: empty
κήρυγμα, -ατος, τό: a proclamation, public notice
ληρέω: to speak or act foolishly
ναός, ναῶ, ὁ: a temple
ὄνομα, τό: name
ὁπόσος: how many
παρακούω: to hear beside
πόλις, ἡ: a city
στήλη, ἡ: a stele, monument
τάφος, ὁ: a funeral mound
χόω: to throw or heap up
ψήφισμα, -ατος, τό: a resolution

μὴ ἀναπλάττειν: pres. inf. after προειπεῖν, "warn *not to fashion*"

περὶ ὧν: the relative is attracted into the case of its antecedent, "*about (that) which* they know"

ἠξιώθησαν: aor. pass., "as many as *have been deemed worthy of*" + gen.

καθαιρεθῆναι: aor. pass. inf. of κατα-αἱρέω, "(resolved) that their statues *be taken down*"

ἐντεθῆναι: aor. pass. inf. of ἐν-τίθημι, that (others) *be installed*"

χῶσαι ... ἐπιστῆσαι: aor. inf., "that the city *heap up* a funeral mound ... *set up* a stele"

ἢν δέ τις παρακούσῃ ... μὴ ἐθελήσῃ: aor. subj. in present general protases, "if someone hears ... and does not wish"

ἐρήμην: cognate acc. with καταδιαιτησάτωσαν, "render a *judgement by default*" i.e. a forfeit

καταδιαιτησάτωσαν: aor. 3 pl. imper. serving as an apodosis, "let them make a judgement!"

ΖΕΥΣ: Δικαιότατον, ὦ Μῶμε· καὶ ὅτῳ δοκεῖ, ἀνατεινάτω
τὴν χεῖρα· μᾶλλον δέ, οὕτω γιγνέσθω, πλείους γὰρ οἶδ᾽
ὅτι ἔσονται οἱ μὴ χειροτονήσοντες. ἀλλὰ νῦν μὲν ἄπιτε·
ὁπόταν δὲ κηρύξῃ ὁ Ἑρμῆς, ἥκετε κομίζοντες ἕκαστος
ἐναργῆ τὰ γνωρίσματα καὶ σαφεῖς τὰς ἀποδείξεις,
πατρὸς ὄνομα καὶ μητρός, καὶ ὅθεν καὶ ὅπως θεὸς

ἀνατείνω: to stretch up, hold up
ἀπόδειξις, -εως, ἡ: a proof
γνώρισμα, τό: a mark, token
δίκαιος: well-ordered, just
δοκέω: to seem good
ἕκαστος, -η, -ον: each, each one
ἐναργής, -ές: visible, palpable
ἥκω: to have come, be present
κηρύττω: to proclaim

κομίζω: to take care of, provide for
μήτηρ, μητρός, ἡ: a mother
ὅθεν: from where, whence
ὄνομα, τό: a name
πατήρ, ὁ: a father
πλείων, -ον: more
σαφής, -ές: clear, plain
χείρ, -ρος, ἡ: the hand
χειροτονέω: to stretch out the hand

ἀνατεινάτω: aor. imper. 3 s., "let each raise his hand!" i.e. to vote

γιγνέσθω: pres. imper. 3 s., "*let it be* so!" i.e. the resolution is passed

πλείους: nom. pred., "will be *more*"

οἱ μὴ χειροτονήσοντες: fut. part. attrib., "those who will not stretch out the hand"
   i.e. will vote against

ἄπιτε: pres. imper., "go away!"

κηρύξῃ: aor. subj. in general temporal clause, "whenever Hermes *makes the
   proclamation*"

ἐναργῆ: neut. pl. acc. pred., "tokens that are *distinct*"

σαφεῖς: f. pl. acc. pred., "proofs that are *clear*"

ἐγένετο, καὶ φυλὴν καὶ φράτορας. ὡς ὅστις ἂν μὴ ταῦτα παράσχηται, οὐδὲν μελήσει τοῖς ἐπιγνώμοσιν εἰ νεών τις μέγαν ἐν τῇ γῇ ἔχει καὶ οἱ ἄνθρωποι θεὸν αὐτὸν εἶναι νομίζουσιν.

γῆ, ἡ: earth
ἐπιγνώμων, -ονος, ὁ: an arbiter
μέλω: to be an object of care
νεώς, -ώ, ὁ: a temple

νομίζω: to consider, believe
παρέχω: to furnish, provide
φράτωρ, -ορος, ὁ: a clan
φυλή, ἡ: a tribe

φυλὴν καὶ φράτορας: a *phratery* is a subdivision of a *phyle* and was a requirement for citizenship in Athens

παράσχηται: aor. subj. of παρα-ἔχω in general relative clause, "whoever does not *provide*"

μελήσει: fut. impersonal, "it will not matter to" + dat.

εἰ ... ἔχει ... νομίζουσιν: ind. question after μελήσει, "matter *whether* someone *has* ... *whether* men *believe*"

θεὸν: acc. pred., "him to be a *god*"

List of Verbs

List of Verbs

The following is a list of verbs that have some irregularity in their conjugation. Contract verbs and other verbs that are completely predictable (-ίζω, -εύω, etc.) are generally not included. The principal parts of the Greek verb in order are 1. Present 2. Future 3. Aorist 4. Perfect Active 5. Perfect Middle 6. Aorist Passive, 7. Future Passive. We have not included the future passive below, since it is very rare. For many verbs not all forms are attested or are only poetic. Verbs are alphabetized under their main stem, followed by various compounds that occur in the *Assembly of the Gods*, with a brief definition. A dash (-) before a form means that it occurs only or chiefly with a prefix. The list is based on the list of verbs in H. Smyth, *A Greek Grammar*.

ἄγω: to lead ἄξω, 2 aor. ἤγαγον, ἦχα, ἦγμαι, ἤχθην
    ἀνάγω: to lead up
    ἐπάγω: to bring on, charge
    συνάγω: to bring together

αἱρέω: to take αἱρήσω, 2 aor. εἷλον, ᾕρηκα, ᾕρημαι, ᾑρέθην
    καθαιρέω: to take down, reduce

ἀκούω: to hear ἀκούσομαι, ἤκουσα, 2 perf. ἀκήκοα, ἠκούσθην
    παρακούω: to hear beside

ἅπτω: to fasten, (mid.) to touch ἅψω, ἧψα, ἧμμαι, ἥφθην
    καθάπτω: to fasten, fix or put upon

βαίνω: to step βήσομαι, 2 aor. ἔβην, βέβηκα
    ἐπιβαίνω: to go upon, trample

βάλλω: to throw βαλῶ, 2 aor. ἔβαλον, βέβληκα, βέβλημαι, ἐβλήθην
    καταβάλλω: to throw down, proscribe

γελάω: to laugh γελάσομαι, ἐγέλασα, ἐγελάσθην
    καταγελάω: to laugh at, jeer

γι(γ)νώσκω: to know γνώσομαι, ἔγνων, ἔγνωκα, ἔγνωσμαι, ἐγνώσθην
    ἀναγιγνώσκω: to read out

γί(γ)νομαι: to become γενήσομαι, 2 aor. ἐγενόμην, 2 perf. γέγονα,
    γεγένημαι, ἐγενήθην

37

γράφω: to write γράψω, ἔγραψα, γέγραφα, γέγραμμαι, ἐγράφην
 παρεγγράφω: to enroll illegally
 συγγράφω: to write, note down

δοκέω: to think, seem δόξω, ἔδοξα, δέδογμαι

ἐθέλω: to wish ἐθελήσω, ἠθέλησα, ἠθέληκα

ἐλέγχω examine, confute: ἐλέγξω, ἤλεγξα, ἐλήλεγμαι, ἠλέγχθην

ἐράω: to love, imp. ἤρων aor. ἠράσθην

ἐρωτάω: to ask ἐρήσομαι, 2 aor. ἠρόμην

ἔρχομαι: to come or go to, fut. εἶμι, 2 aor. ἦλθον, 2 perf. ἐλήλυθα
 παρέρχομαι: to advance

ἔχω: to have ἕξω, 2 aor. ἔσχον, ἔσχηκα, imperf. εἶχον
 ἀνέχω: to hold back
 μετέχω: to partake of
 παρέχω: to furnish, provide, supply

καλύπτω: to cover καλύψω, ἐκάλυψα, κεκάλυμμαι, ἐκαλύφθην
 ἐπικαλύπτω: to cover up

κηρυττω: to proclaim, κηρύξω ἐκήρυξα, -κεκήρυχα, κεκήρυγμαι, ἐκηρυχθην

κρίνω: to decide κρινῶ, ἔκρινα, κέκρικα, κέκριμαι, ἐκρίθην
 ἐκκρίνω: to choose

λαμβάνω: to take λήψομαι, ἔλαβον, εἴληφα, εἴλημμαι, ἐλήφθην
 ξυλλαμβάνω: to capture

λανθάνω: to escape notice λήσω, ἔλαθον, λέληθα
 διαλανθάνω: to escape notice

λέγω: to speak ἐρέω, εἶπον, εἴρηκα, λέλεγμαι, ἐλέχθην and ἐρρήθην

λείπω: to leave λείψω, ἔλιπον, λέλοιπα, λέλειμμαι, ἐλείφθην
 ἐπιλείπω: to leave behind, run low

ὁράω: to see ὄψομαι, 2 aor. εἶδον, ἑώρακα, ὤφθην, imperf. ἑώρων

πείθω: to persuade πείσω, ἔπεισα, 2 perf. πέποιθα, πέπεισμαι, ἐπείσθην

πίνω: to drink πίομαι, 2 aor. ἔπιον, πέπωκα, -πέπομαι, -επόθην
 προπίνω: to toast

πίπτω: to fall πεσοῦμαι, 2 aor. ἔπεσον, πέπτωκα
 ἐμπίπτω: fall upon

πλάττω: to form ἔπλασα, πέπλασμαι, ἐπλάσθην
 ἀναπλάττω: to remodel

πνέω: to blow πνεύσομαι, ἔπνευσα, -πέπνευκα
 ἀποπνέω: to breathe forth

πράττω: to do πράξω, ἔπραξα, 2 perf. πέπραχα, πέπραγμαι, ἐπράχθην

ῥιπτω: to throw ῥίψω, ἔρριψα, 2 perf. ἔρριφα, ἔρριμμαι, ἐρρίφην
  ἀπορρίπτω: to throw away, put away

στέλλω: to send, arrange στελῶ, ἔστειλα, -έσταλκα, ἔσταλμαι, ἐστάλην
  ὑποστέλλω: to hold back

στρέφω: to turn στρέψω, ἔστρεψα, ἔστραμμαι, ἐστρέφθην
  συστρέφω: to curl up

τάττω: to arrange, τάξω, ἔταξα, 2 perf. τέταχα, τέταγμαι, ἐτάχθην
  ἐπιτάττω: to put upon, establish

τείνω: stretch τενῶ, -έτεινα, -τέτακα, τέταμαι, -ετάθην
  ἀνατείνω: to stretch up, hold up

τρέπω: to turn τρέψω, ἔτρεψα, τέτροφα, ἐτράπην
  ἐπιτρέπω: to turn towards, allow

φαίνω: to show, to appear (*mid.*) φανῶ, ἔφηνα, πέφηνα, πέφασμαι, ἐφάνην
  ἀποφαίνω: to show forth, display, assert, declare

φέρω: to bear οἴσω, 1 aor. ἤνεγκα, 2 aor. ἤνεγκον, 2 perf. ἐνήνοχα, perf.
  mid. ἐνήνεγμαι, aor. pass. ἠνέχθην
  διαφέρω: to be superior to

φύω: to bring forth φύσω, ἔφυσα, 2 aor. ἔφυν, πέφυκα
  ὑποφύω: to make to grow up

χαίρω: to rejoice at χαιρήσω, κεχάρηκα, κεχάρημαι, ἐχάρην

χαλεπαίνω: to be offended χαλεπανῶ, ἐχαλέπηνα, ἐχαλεπάνθην

χέω: to pour fut. χέω, aor. ἔχεα, κέχυκα, κέχυμαι, ἐχύθην
  περιχέω: to pour round or over

ψεύδω: to lie ψεύσω, ἔψευσα, ἔψευσμαι, ἐψεύσθην

ὠθέω: to push ὤσω, ἔωσα, ἔωσμαι, ἐώσθην
  παρωθέω: to push aside

Glossary

A α

ἀγαθός, -ή, -όν: good

ἄγω: to lead or carry, to convey, bring

ἀεί: always

ἀκούω: to hear

ἀληθής, -ές: unconcealed, true

ἀλλά: otherwise, but

ἀλλήλων: one another

ἄλλος, -η, -ον: another, other

ἄλλως: in another way

ἄν: (*indefinite particle; generalizes dependent clauses with subjunctive; indicates contrary-to-fact with independent clauses in the indicative; potentiality with the optative*)

ἀντί: in return for, instead of (+ *gen.*)

ἀξιόω: to ask

ἅπας, ἅπασα, ἅπαν: all, the whole

αὐτός, -ή, -ό: he, she, it; self, same

ἀπό: from, away from (+ *gen.*)

Γ γ

γάρ: for

γε: at least, at any rate (*postpositive*)

γί(γ)νομαι: to become, happen, occur

γί(γ)νώσκω: to know

γοῦν: at least then, at any rate, any way

γυνή, γυναικός, ἡ: a woman, wife

Δ δ

δέ: and, but, on the other hand (*preceded by* μέν)

δεῖ: it is necessary

διά: through (+ *gen.*); with, by means of (+ *acc.*)

δίδωμι: to give

δοκέω: to seem

E ε

ἐγώ, μου: I, my

ἐθέλω: to will, wish, purpose

εἰ: if

εἶπον: to say (*aor.*)

εἷς, μία, ἕν: one

εἶτα: next, then

ἐκ, ἐξ: from, out of, after (+ *gen.*)

ἕκαστος, -η, -ον: each, every

ἐκεῖνος, -η, -ον: that, that one

ἐμός, -ή, -όν: mine

ἐν: in, at, among (+ *dat.*)

ἕνεκα, ἕνεκεν: for the sake of (+ *gen.*)

ἔοικα: to seem, to be like

ἐπί: at (+ *gen.*); on, upon (+ *dat.*); on to, against (+ *acc.*)

ἔρχομαι: to go

ἐς: to, into (+ *acc.*)

ἔτι: still

εὖ: well, thoroughly

ἔχω: to have; to be able (+ *inf.*)

H η

ἤ: or; than

ἤδη: already, now

ἥκω: to have come, be present, be here

ἦλθον: to go (*aor.*)

ἡμεῖς, ἡμῶν, ἡμᾶς, ἡμῖν: we, us

Θ θ

θεός, θεοῦ, ὁ/ἡ: a god, goddess

I ι

ἴσος, -η, -ον: equal to, the same as

K κ

καί: and, also, even

κατά, καθ': down, along, according to (+ *acc.*)

43

Λ λ

λέγω: to speak, say, tell
λόγος, ὁ: a word

Μ μ

μάλιστα; very much, especially
μᾶλλον: more, rather
μέγας, μέγαλα, μέγα: great, large
μηδείς, μηδεμία, μηδέν: no one, nothing
μέν: on the one hand (*followed by* δέ)
μετά: with (+ *gen.*); after (+ *acc.*)
μή: not, lest, don't (+ *subj. or imper.*)
μηδέ: but not, and not, nor
μήτε: and not; **μήτε...μήτε**: neither... nor
μόνος, -η, -ον: alone, only

Ν ν

νῦν, νυνί: now, at this moment

Ο ο

ὁ, ἡ, τό: the (*definite article*)
ὅς, ἥ, ὅ: who, which (*relative pronoun*)
οἶδα: to know (*perf.*)
οἷος, -α, -ον: such as, what sort
ὀλίγος, -η, -ον: few, little, small
ὅλος, -η, -ον: whole, entire
ὅμως: nevertheless, all the same
ὄνομα, -ατος, τό: a name
ὀξύς, -εῖα, -ύ: sharp, acute, keen
ὅποταν: whenever (+ *subj.*)
ὅπως: as, in such manner as, how
ὁράω: to see
ὅσπερ, ἥπερ, ὅπερ: the very one who
ὅστις, ὅτι: anyone who, anything which
ὅτι: that, because
οὐ, οὐκ, οὐχ: not
οὐδέ: but not
οὐδείς, οὐδεμία, οὐδέν: no one

οὐκοῦν: therefore, then, accordingly
οὖν: so, therefore
οὐρανός, ὁ: heaven
οὔτε: and not; **οὔτε...οὔτε**: neither...nor
οὗτος, αὕτη, τοῦτο: this

Π π

παῖς, παιδός, ὁ: a child
πάνυ: altogether, entirely
παρά: from (+ *gen.*); beside (+ *dat.*); to (+ *acc.*)
πᾶς, πᾶσα, πᾶν: all, every, whole
περί: concerning, about (+ *gen.*); about, around (+ *acc.*)
πλήν: unless, but
ποιέω: to make, do
πολύς, πολλή, πολύ: many, much
που: somewhere
ποῦ: where?
πρός: to, near (+ *dat.*), from (+ *gen.*), towards (+ *acc.*)
πῶς: how? in what way?
πως: somehow, in some way

Σ σ

σύ, σοῦ, σέ, σοί: you (*singular*)

Τ τ

τε: and (*postpositive*)
τις, τι: someone, something (*indefinite*)
τίς, τί: who? which? (*interrogative*)
τοιοῦτος, -αύτη, -οῦτο: such as this
τοσοῦτος, -αύτη, -οῦτο: of such a kind, so large, so great

Υ υ

ὑμεῖς, ὑμῶν, ὑμᾶς, ὑμῖν: you (*plural*)
υἱός, ὁ: a son
ὑπό, ὑφ': from under, by (+ *gen.*); under (+ *dat.*); toward (+ *acc.*)

Φ φ

φέρω: to bear, endure

φημί: to say

Χ χ

χείρ, χειρός, ἡ: a hand

χρή: it is necessary

Ω ω

ὦ: oh! (*vocative*)

ὡς: (*adv.*) as, so, how; (*conj.*) that, in order that, since; (*prep.*) to (*+ acc.*); as if, as (*+ part.*); as _____ as possible (*superlative*)

NOTES

NOTES

NOTES

Made in the USA
Middletown, DE
12 May 2015